TEST SUCCESS

GRADE **6**

C0-BWW-123

Targeting the
TAKS
Reading · Writing · Mathematics

Photo Credits:
p. 23 ©Bettmann/CORBIS; p. 24 ©Horace Pippin, Zachariah, 1943. Oil on canvas, 11x14". Courtesy The Butler Institute of American Art, Youngstown, Ohio; p. 37 ©Hulton-Deutsch Collection/CORBIS; pp. 53, 54, 59, 60 ©Brown Brothers; p. 71 ©Koren Ziv/CORBIS SYGMA.

The Texas Education Agency, the publisher of the Texas Assessment of Knowledge and Skills, has neither endorsed nor authorized this test-preparation book.

ISBN: 0-7398-9737-3

Harcourt Achieve
Rigby · Steck-Vaughn

www.HarcourtAchieve.com
1.800.531.5015

Printed in the United States of America.
1 2 3 4 5 6 7 8 9 073 09 08 07 06 05 04

Table of Contents

A brief description of the types of test questions is given to prepare students with what to expect on the 6th-grade TAKS in Reading and 7th-grade TAKS in Writing.

The four TAKS reading objectives for 6th grade and the six TAKS writing objectives for 7th grade are listed with explanations. Students should review these objectives before beginning their work in this section.

MODELED INSTRUCTION

This part of the book is divided into smaller portions of the 6th-grade reading test and the 7th-grade writing test. Hints are provided to guide students toward the correct responses.

Test-taking strategies are provided to help students perform their best when taking the TAKS in Reading and the TAKS in Writing.

TESTS

The reading test and the writing test provide students with an opportunity to practice the skills detailed in Modeled Instruction. These tests are designed to simulate the actual 6th-grade TAKS in Reading and the 7th-grade TAKS in Writing.

TO THE STUDENT

A brief description of the types of test problems is given to prepare students with what to expect on the 6th-grade TAKS in Mathematics.

The six TAKS mathematics objectives for 6th grade are listed. Students should review these objectives before beginning their work in this section.

MODELED INSTRUCTION

This part of the book is divided into six units based on the objectives covered on the 6th-grade TAKS in Mathematics. Hints are provided to guide students toward the correct responses.

Test-taking strategies are provided to help students perform their best when taking the TAKS in Mathematics.

This test provides students with an opportunity to practice the skills detailed in Modeled Instruction. It is designed to simulate the actual 6th-grade TAKS in Mathematics.

Answers are provided to all the questions and problems in the Modeled Instruction and Test sections of the book. These answers are correlated to the specific objective, knowledge and skills statement, and student expectation that the item assesses.

These charts are provided to help you track your child's strengths and weaknesses in terms of the TAKS objectives.

Answers for the test portion of Section A: Reading and Writing should be recorded on this page.

Answers for the test portion of Section B: Mathematics should be recorded on this page.

A chart is provided for student use throughout the Mathematics Modeled Instruction and Test sections. This chart is designed according to the chart that is used on the 6th-grade TAKS in Mathematics.

Dear Parent or Educator,

Welcome to **Targeting the TAKS**. You have selected a book that will help your child develop the skills he or she needs to succeed on the TAKS when required to take the reading and math tests in sixth grade and the writing test in seventh grade.

Although testing can be a source of anxiety for children, this book will give your child the preparation and practice that he or she needs to feel better prepared and more confident when taking the TAKS. Research shows that children who are acquainted with the scoring format of standardized tests score higher on those tests. Students also score higher when they practice and understand the skills and objectives covered on the test.

This book has many features that will help you prepare your child to take the TAKS:

- Explanation and listing of the TAKS objectives geared both for the parent and for the child
- Scoring rubric used for the written part of the TAKS
- Modeled instruction for the child about how to answer test questions and hints to guide the child toward the correct response
- Test-taking tips
- Tests that simulate the actual TAKS tests
- A complete answer key, including references to the specific TAKS objective being tested on each question
- A correlation of the TAKS objectives to the questions
- An evaluation chart to map your child's performance on the Test sections of the book. You can use this chart to pinpoint areas where your child may need extra practice.

If your child expresses anxiety about taking a test or completing these lessons, help him or her understand what causes the stress. Then, talk about ways to eliminate anxiety. Above all, enjoy this time you spend with your child. He or she will feel your support, and test scores will improve as success in test taking is experienced.

Help your child maintain a positive attitude about taking a standardized test such as the TAKS. Let your child know that each test provides an opportunity to shine.

Sincerely,

The Educators and Staff of

Harcourt School Supply

P.S. You might want to visit our website at www.HarcourtSchoolSupply.com for more test preparation materials as well as additional review of content areas.

TO THE PARENT

This section of the book is designed to ensure peak performance on the Texas Assessment of Knowledge and Skills in Reading and Writing. By offering grade-specific instruction, test-taking tips, and authentic practice, this book will help your child approach the 6th-grade TAKS in Reading and the 7th-grade TAKS in Writing strategically and confidently.

This section includes content and draws questions from the Texas Essential Knowledge and Skills (TEKS) for Grade 6 English. The first part of the reading and writing section contains modeled instruction with hints to guide students. The second part of the reading and writing section contains two practice tests that closely resemble the actual 6th-grade TAKS in Reading and 7th-grade TAKS in Writing.

The following are descriptions of the reading and writing tests.

Reading: The reading test contains four types of selections—a narrative selection, an expository selection, a mixed selection, and a paired selection. The mixed selection combines two types of writing in a single passage. The paired selection links two separate passages that share a common theme. After each selection, students will be given a series of multiple-choice items.

Writing: The writing test consists of two parts: revising and editing and a written composition. In the revising and editing part, students will be given passages that have errors in grammar, punctuation, spelling, and organization. After these passages, students will be given a series of multiple-choice items that test revising and editing skills. For the written composition, students must write a composition in response to a writing prompt.

Throughout the entire administration of the 7th-grade TAKS in Writing, each student must have access to a dictionary. At least one dictionary will be provided per every five students during the TAKS. Dictionaries may be provided by the school or students may bring their own. Any dictionary, other than one that contains a separate grammar guide, is acceptable. However, more current dictionaries are preferable because of the special features offered (such as synonyms, idiomatic expressions, geographical names, and biographical names). Use of dictionary/thesaurus combinations as well as stand-alone thesauruses will also be permitted during the Writing test. In order to best prepare your child for the TAKS, dictionaries and thesauruses, or dictionary/thesaurus combinations, should be provided when administering the practice Writing test in the Student Book.

The TAKS in Reading will include only multiple-choice items. The TAKS in Writing will include two types of questions: multiple-choice items and a writing prompt.

Multiple-choice Items: The multiple-choice items are always followed by four answer choices. In the Modeled Instruction section, students mark their answers by filling in the circles at the bottom of the page. In the Test section, students mark their answers on a separate answer sheet.

Writing Prompt: There is only one writing prompt in the 7th-grade TAKS in Writing. The writing prompt will require students to respond with a written composition. Students may address the writing prompt in any way they choose except in the form of poetry. Two lined pages are provided for student compositions. Students may not write outside the boxes that enclose the lines and will not be given additional pages to write their compositions. It is important that all students write their compositions neatly and legibly; however, each student may choose whether to write in cursive or print. Students will be allowed to do some prewriting before composing a final answer.

Written Composition Scoring and Rubric

The written composition will be scored for rhetorical effectiveness (Objective 1) and for conventions of standard written English (Objective 2). While student compositions will be graded as a whole, the 4-point rubric scoring will rely heavily on the evaluation of several specific elements within the composition. The specific elements examined will include appropriate and accurate response to the prompt, logical progression of ideas, focus and coherence, depth of development, sustained voice, and overall command of conventions.

The overall command of conventions in a composition will be judged holistically and not upon the number of errors. Students will be penalized more severely for convention errors that affect the clarity of the composition. In addition, attempts at sophisticated construction of sentences and/or use of words will be taken into account in the scoring of conventions.

4-point Rubric for Written Composition

4	**Exemplary response**
	• appropriate and accurate response to the prompt
	• logical progression of ideas
	• focused and coherent
	• fully developed
	• sustained voice throughout
	• a superior command of conventions
3	**Sufficient response**
	• appropriate and accurate response to the prompt
	• logical progression of ideas
	• primarily focused and generally coherent
	• sufficiently developed
	• sustained voice through most of composition
	• a fair command of conventions
2	**Partially sufficient response**
	• somewhat appropriate and somewhat accurate response to the prompt
	• logical progression of ideas not always present
	• somewhat focused and somewhat coherent
	• lacking full development
	• does not sustain voice throughout most of composition
	• a weak command of conventions
1	**Insufficient response**
	• inappropriate and inaccurate response to the prompt
	• logical progression of ideas not present
	• lacking focus and coherence
	• lacking development
	• no sustained voice
	• no command of conventions

Introduction to the TAKS Reading and Writing Objectives

Included on the following pages are the four objectives designed specifically for the 6th-grade TAKS in Reading and the six objectives designed specifically for the 7th-grade TAKS in Writing. Within each objective is a more specific breakdown of the knowledge and skills statements (which organize the objective) and the student expectations (or relevant TEKS that fit under that objective).

When preparing your child for the TAKS in Reading and the TAKS in Writing, it is important to accurately interpret the TAKS objectives and the information they encompass. This can be somewhat difficult, due to the complex organization of a large amount of information. An excerpt from Objective 4 of the 6th-grade Reading TAKS objectives has been provided below to illustrate the breakdown of each objective into three parts.

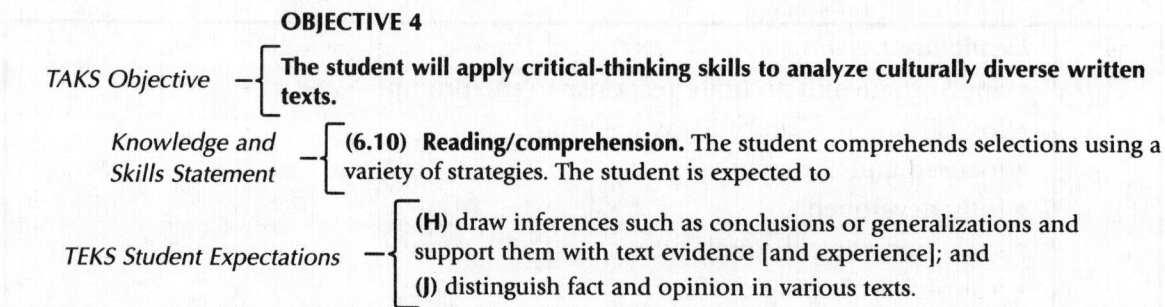

OBJECTIVE 4

TAKS Objective — **The student will apply critical-thinking skills to analyze culturally diverse written texts.**

Knowledge and Skills Statement — **(6.10) Reading/comprehension.** The student comprehends selections using a variety of strategies. The student is expected to

TEKS Student Expectations — **(H)** draw inferences such as conclusions or generalizations and support them with text evidence [and experience]; and
(J) distinguish fact and opinion in various texts.

The knowledge and skills statements broadly indicate the knowledge each student must attain and the skills he or she must master in order to successfully meet the TAKS evaluative criteria. The number found before each statement is the same identifying number of the statement in the TEKS. The "6" at the beginning of each number indicates that the knowledge and skills being tested are on the 6th-grade English level.

The TEKS student expectations outline exactly what a student must accomplish in order to demonstrate proficiency in the TAKS objectives and tests. However, students will not be tested on all the information contained in each expectation. Any information contained in brackets will not be tested on the TAKS. See student expectation **(H)** in the sample above for an example of this exception. In addition, when the term *such as* is employed in a student expectation, it implies that the information following may or may not be tested, and that other information similar to that given may be assessed on the TAKS test. When the term *including* is used, it is far more likely that all information following will be assessed, though additional information similar to that given may also be tested on the TAKS.

On pages 10–15 is a detailed description of each of the four Reading TAKS objectives and the six Writing TAKS objectives that will be assessed on the 6th-grade TAKS in Reading and 7th-grade TAKS in Writing. These descriptions will help you prepare your child for the TAKS. The descriptions will also help you assess your child's strengths and weaknesses as he or she works through the book.

On page 18 is a description of the objectives addressed to your child. You may wish to go over these objectives with your child.

READING OBJECTIVES

OBJECTIVE 1

The student will demonstrate a basic understanding of culturally diverse written texts.

(6.9) Reading/vocabulary development. The student acquires an extensive vocabulary through reading and systematic word study. The student is expected to

(B) draw on experiences to bring meanings to words in context such as interpreting [idioms,] multiple-meaning words, and analogies;
(D) determine meanings of derivatives by applying knowledge of the meanings of root words such as *like*, *pay*, or *happy* and affixes such as *dis-*, *pre-*, or *un-*; and
(F) distinguish denotative and connotative meanings.

(6.10) Reading/comprehension. The student comprehends selections using a variety of strategies. The student is expected to

(F) determine a text's main (or major) ideas and how those ideas are supported with details; and
(G) paraphrase and summarize text to recall, inform, or organize ideas.

OBJECTIVE 2

The student will apply knowledge of literary elements to understand culturally diverse written texts.

(6.12) Reading/text structures/literary concepts. The student analyzes the characteristics of various types of texts (genres). The student is expected to

(F) analyze characters, including their traits, motivations, conflicts, points of view, relationships, and changes they undergo;
(G) recognize and analyze story plot, setting, and problem resolution; and
(J) recognize and interpret literary devices such as flashback, foreshadowing, and symbolism.

OBJECTIVE 3

The student will use a variety of strategies to analyze culturally diverse written texts.

(6.10) Reading/comprehension. The student comprehends selections using a variety of strategies. The student is expected to

(E) use the text's structure or progression of ideas such as cause and effect or chronology to locate and recall information;
(I) find similarities and differences across texts such as in treatment, scope, or organization; and
(L) represent text information in different ways such as in outline, timeline, or graphic organizer.

(6.12) Reading/text structures/literary concepts. The student analyzes the characteristics of various types of texts (genres). The student is expected to

(A) identify the purposes of different types of texts such as to inform, influence, express, or entertain;

(C) compare communication in different forms such as [contrasting a dramatic performance with a print version of the same story or] comparing story variants; and

(H) describe how the author's perspective or point of view affects the text.

OBJECTIVE 4

The student will apply critical-thinking skills to analyze culturally diverse written texts.

(6.10) Reading/comprehension. The student comprehends selections using a variety of strategies. The student is expected to

(H) draw inferences such as conclusions or generalizations and support them with text evidence [and experience]; and

(J) distinguish fact and opinion in various texts.

(6.11) Reading/literary response. The student expresses and supports responses to various types of texts. The student is expected to

(C) support responses by referring to relevant aspects of text [and his/her own experiences]; and

(D) connect, compare, and contrast ideas, themes, and issues across text.

(6.12) Reading/text structures/literary concepts. The student analyzes the characteristics of various types of texts (genres). The student is expected to

(I) analyze ways authors organize and present ideas such as through cause/effect, compare/contrast, inductively, deductively, or chronologically; and

(K) recognize how style, tone, and mood contribute to the effect of the text.

11

WRITING OBJECTIVES

OBJECTIVE 1

The student will, within a given context, produce an effective composition for a specific purpose.

> **(7.15) Writing/purposes.** The student writes for a variety of audiences and purposes and in a variety of forms. The student is expected to
>
>> **(A)** write to express, [discover, record,] develop, reflect on ideas, and to problem solve;
>> **(B)** write to influence such as to persuade, argue, and request;
>> **(C)** write to inform such as to explain, describe, report, and narrate;
>> **(D)** write to entertain such as to compose [humorous poems or] short stories;
>> **(E)** select and use voice and style appropriate to audience and purpose;
>> **(G)** use literary devices effectively such as suspense, dialogue, and figurative language; and
>> **(H)** produce cohesive and coherent written texts by organizing ideas, using effective transitions, and choosing precise wording.
>
> **(7.16) Writing/penmanship/capitalization/punctuation/spelling.** The student composes original texts, applying the conventions of written language such as capitalization, punctuation, handwriting, penmanship, and spelling to communicate clearly. The student is expected to
>
>> **(A)** write legibly by selecting cursive or manuscript as appropriate.
>
> **(7.18) Writing/writing processes.** The student selects and uses writing processes for self-initiated and assigned writing. The student is expected to
>
>> **(C)** revise selected drafts by adding, elaborating, deleting, combining, and rearranging text; and
>> **(D)** revise drafts for coherence, progression, and logical support of ideas.

OBJECTIVE 2

The student will produce a piece of writing that demonstrates a command of the conventions of spelling, capitalization, punctuation, grammar, usage, and sentence structure.

> **(7.16) Writing/penmanship/capitalization/punctuation/spelling.** The student composes original texts, applying the conventions of written language such as capitalization, punctuation, handwriting, penmanship, and spelling to communicate clearly. The student is expected to
>
>> **(B)** capitalize and punctuate correctly to clarify and enhance meaning such as capitalizing titles, using hyphens, semicolons, colons, possessives, and sentence punctuation;
>> **(C)** spell derivatives correctly by applying the spellings of bases and affixes;

(D) spell frequently misspelled words correctly such as *their*, *they're*, and *there*;

(E) use resources to find correct spellings; and

(F) spell accurately in final drafts.

(7.17) Writing/grammar/usage. The student applies standard grammar and usage to communicate clearly and effectively in writing. The student is expected to

(A) write in complete sentences, varying the types such as compound and complex sentences, and use appropriately punctuated independent and dependent clauses;

(B) use conjunctions to connect ideas meaningfully;

(C) employ standard English usage in writing for audiences, including subject-verb agreement, pronoun referents, and parts of speech;

(D) use adjectives (comparative and superlative forms) and adverbs appropriately to make writing vivid or precise;

(E) use prepositional phrases to elaborate written ideas;

(F) use verb tenses appropriately and consistently such as present, past, future, perfect, and progressive;

(G) write with increasing accuracy when using apostrophes in contractions such as *won't* and possessives such as *Smith's*; and

(H) write with increasing accuracy when using pronoun case such as "She had the party."

(7.18) Writing/writing processes. The student selects and uses writing processes for self-initiated and assigned writing. The student is expected to

(E) edit drafts for specific purposes such as to ensure standard usage, varied sentence structure, and appropriate word choice; and

(H) proofread his/her own writing and that of others.

OBJECTIVE 3

The student will recognize appropriate organization of ideas in written text.

(7.18) Writing/writing processes. The student selects and uses writing processes for self-initiated and assigned writing. The student is expected to

(C) revise selected drafts by adding, elaborating, deleting, combining, and rearranging text; and

(D) revise drafts for coherence, progression, and logical support of ideas.

13

OBJECTIVE 4

The student will recognize correct and effective sentence construction in written text.

(7.17) Writing/grammar/usage. The student applies standard grammar and usage to communicate clearly and effectively in writing. The student is expected to

(A) write in complete sentences, varying the types such as compound and complex sentences, and use appropriately punctuated independent and dependent clauses;

(B) use conjunctions to connect ideas meaningfully; and

(E) use prepositional phrases to elaborate written ideas.

(7.18) Writing/writing processes. The student selects and uses writing processes for self-initiated and assigned writing. The student is expected to

(E) edit drafts for specific purposes such as to ensure standard usage, varied sentence structure, and appropriate word choice.

OBJECTIVE 5

The student will recognize standard usage and appropriate word choice in written text.

(7.17) Writing/grammar/usage. The student applies standard grammar and usage to communicate clearly and effectively in writing. The student is expected to

(C) employ standard English usage in writing for audiences, including subject-verb agreement, pronoun referents, and parts of speech;

(D) use adjectives (comparative and superlative forms) and adverbs appropriately to make writing vivid or precise;

(F) use verb tenses appropriately and consistently such as present, past, future, perfect, and progressive; and

(H) write with increasing accuracy when using pronoun case such as "She had the party."

(7.18) Writing/writing processes. The student selects and uses writing processes for self-initiated and assigned writing. The student is expected to

(E) edit drafts for specific purposes such as to ensure standard usage, varied sentence structure, and appropriate word choice; and

(H) proofread his/her own writing and that of others.

OBJECTIVE 6

The student will proofread for correct punctuation, capitalization, and spelling in written text.

(7.16) Writing/penmanship/capitalization/punctuation/spelling. The student composes original texts, applying the conventions of written language such as capitalization, punctuation, handwriting, penmanship, and spelling to communicate clearly. The student is expected to

(B) capitalize and punctuate correctly to clarify and enhance meaning such as capitalizing titles, using hyphens, semicolons, colons, possessives, and sentence punctuation;

(C) spell derivatives correctly by applying the spellings of bases and affixes;

(D) spell frequently misspelled words correctly such as *their*, *they're*, and *there*; and

(F) spell accurately in final drafts.

(7.17) Writing/grammar/usage. The student applies standard grammar and usage to communicate clearly and effectively in writing. The student is expected to

(G) write with increasing accuracy when using apostrophes in contractions such as *won't* and possessives such as *Smith's*.

(7.18) Writing/writing processes. The student selects and uses writing processes for self-initiated and assigned writing. The student is expected to

(H) proofread his/her own writing and that of others.

TO THE STUDENT

This section of the book provides practice for two tests: the 6th-grade TAKS in Reading and the 7th-grade TAKS in Writing. The objectives for these tests are listed on page 18 of this book.

Reading

The reading test is made up of different types of selections. These selections may be the following: short stories; newspaper articles; passages about a particular person or event; stories with some facts from history mixed into them; passages that have an advertisement, checklist, or recipe in them; and selections that are made up of two smaller passages that are linked by a common theme. You may find other, similar selections as well. After each selection in the reading test, you must answer some multiple-choice items.

• Multiple-choice Items

The multiple-choice items will be based on the reading selection you just read. Multiple-choice items should be familiar to you. There are four answer choices after each question. Fill in the circle that represents the correct answer choice. Remember to pick the choice that you think is the BEST answer. In the Modeled Instruction section, you must fill in your answer at the bottom of the page. In the Test section, you must fill in your answer on a separate answer sheet, located at the back of this book.

Writing

The writing test is made up of two parts: revising and editing and a written composition. You will be allowed to use a dictionary for both parts of this writing test.

Revising and Editing

In the first part of the writing test, you will be given some passages that look like essays or reports that you or your classmates would write. These passages will have errors in grammar, punctuation, spelling, and organization. After these passages, you will be given some multiple-choice items that test your skills in revising and editing.

- **Multiple-choice Items**

The multiple-choice items will be just like the items in the reading test. But, some questions may have an answer choice that states "Make no change" or "No revision is needed." Fill in the circle for one of these answer choices if the text that the question is asking about does not have any errors and does not need to be changed. In the Modeled Instruction section, fill in your answer at the bottom of the page. In the Test section, fill in your answer on the separate answer sheet.

Written Composition

In the second part of the writing test, you will be given a writing prompt. You must write a composition in response to the prompt.

- **Writing Prompt**

The writing prompt will be a statement telling you to write a composition about something. You can write this composition in any way that you choose EXCEPT by writing a poem.

You are given two pages to do some prewriting before you write your composition. Use these pages to plan what you want to write. You may want to outline your composition or use a graphic organizer.

You are then given two lined pages to write your composition. You must write your entire composition within these two pages. You will not be given more paper if you run out of room, so make sure you plan your composition carefully. You must also write within the box around the lines on each page. Do not write outside of this box when you write your composition.

Your composition will be scored on a scale of 1 to 4. A score of 4 is the best score you can receive.

Reading Objectives

The 6th-grade TAKS for Reading will assess four different reading objectives. These objectives are listed below.

OBJECTIVE 1: The student will demonstrate a basic understanding of culturally diverse written texts.

OBJECTIVE 2: The student will apply knowledge of literary elements to understand culturally diverse written texts.

OBJECTIVE 3: The student will use a variety of strategies to analyze culturally diverse written texts.

OBJECTIVE 4: The student will apply critical-thinking skills to analyze culturally diverse written texts.

Writing Objectives

The 7th-grade TAKS for Writing will assess six different writing objectives. These objectives are listed below.

OBJECTIVE 1: The student will, within a given context, produce an effective composition for a specific purpose.

OBJECTIVE 2: The student will produce a piece of writing that demonstrates a command of the conventions of spelling, capitalization, punctuation, grammar, usage, and sentence structure.

OBJECTIVE 3: The student will recognize appropriate organization of ideas in written text.

OBJECTIVE 4: The student will recognize correct and effective sentence construction in written text.

OBJECTIVE 5: The student will recognize standard usage and appropriate word choice in written text.

OBJECTIVE 6: The student will proofread for correct punctuation, capitalization, and spelling in written text.

Reading

DIRECTIONS: Carefully read the selection. Then answer the questions.

The Soapstone Carver

My notes about what I am reading

1   Aola watched his grandmother shape a piece of soapstone into a hunter, creating a tiny man holding a spear. That part of the sculpture would be delicate, so she worked slowly and deliberately. Aola wondered how his grandmother, small and hunched over, could carve for so many hours. He was a restless boy who enjoyed trapping and fishing with his father. But his father had just left their home in Arctic Bay, Antarctica, to seek a job elsewhere. He sent money so that his family did not have to live in poverty.

2   Like many of the Inuit people, Aola's family did not have much money. That is why his grandmother learned to carve soapstone in the 1960's, when outsiders became interested in the craft. Ever since Aola could remember, his grandmother had been producing these little figures—fish, bears, seal, people—designing whatever the traders considered "authentic." She worked until the skin on her hands peeled. When she became too uncomfortable, she stopped for a while to let her hands heal.

3   Today, Aola's grandmother seemed weary, and her expression was brooding and tense. She worked diligently, but her heart was not in it.

4   "Is something wrong? Have you had bad news?" He braced himself for what he would hear.

5   Grandmother frowned. "You should go and read your schoolbooks. It is almost time to make dinner." Winters were black and <u>frigid</u>, and Aola would not feel free until the sun shone and the Inuit people followed their ancient custom of going to live on the land. In winter, families stayed in the village and made a living as best they could. The children were expected to study, much to Aola's annoyance.

6   "I want to know," Aola persisted. "I am nearly thirteen, no longer a child who has to have frightening things concealed from him."

GO

My notes about what I am reading

7   "Your father has lost his job."

8   Aola understood the significance of her words. There would be less money for clothing, food, and other necessities. Grandmother would have to work much harder until his father could send money. She earned some income from her art, but she could not work as steadily as she had as a young woman. He stared at his grandmother's hands, which looked dry and sore. His own hands, callused from rough play, looked strong and firm. He had heard that Inuit art was valuable in other parts of the world, where it was displayed in galleries and bought by collectors. Aola took a deep breath.

9   "Grandmother, I am ready to learn to carve."

10   His grandmother looked up at him, unprepared for his comment. To his surprise, the elderly woman did not argue with him. Instead, she began talking to him in a way that was unfamiliar.

11   "When you hold a stone, you have to imagine that there is something inside, eager to come out. It is waiting for you to find it. This stone held a hunter, impatient to use his spear. I was tired when I thought about how much effort it would take to dig him out of this piece of stone, but I knew that he was there. So I carved and carved until I saw his shape. Then I had to work with all my skill and attention to make the details come out right."

12   Aola understood. "I want to carve," he reminded her. He did not even know if he meant what he said, but he wanted to earn money to help his family. "Do you have a stone for me?"

13   "You can start with this one," she replied, removing a rough stone from a basket. "What do you see in this piece?"

14   Aola carefully studied the flat, oval stone and envisioned water and movement. "A kayak," he decided.

15   "Good," Grandmother smiled. She chose a tool from her box and very slowly and painstakingly guided his hands over the stone until he felt the blade sink in, starting its long labor.

GO➡

Use "The Soapstone Carver" (pp. 19–20) to answer questions 1–8.

---

1 In paragraph 5, the word <u>frigid</u> is used to communicate a feeling of —

A happiness

B coldness

C terror

D sorrow

💡 **HINT**
Read paragraph 5. What is life like during an Arctic winter?

Objective 1(6.9)(B) – *The student is expected to draw on experiences to bring meanings to words in context such as interpreting [idioms,] multiple-meaning words, and analogies.*

2 Paragraph 2 is important to the story because it —

F explains the factors that caused Grandmother to become an expert soapstone carver

G describes the sudden interest in soapstone carving that emerged in the 1960's

H suggests that Grandmother had to abandon her own goals and dreams in order to support the family

J describes Grandmother's attitude toward the history and art of soapstone carving

💡 **HINT**
What is the main idea of the second paragraph? What does it tell us about Grandmother's motivation for learning to carve soapstone figures?

Objective 2(6.12)(G) – *The student is expected to recognize and analyze story plot, setting, and problem resolution.*

3 In paragraph 4, what does the author mean by the statement, "He braced himself for what he would hear"?

A Aola was eager to learn the latest news from the world beyond his village.

B Aola was furious because his grandmother hesitated to tell him the truth.

C Aola had to prepare himself to hear some unpleasant news.

D Aola was mature enough to discuss any subject with his grandmother.

💡 **HINT**
How does Aola interpret Grandmother's expression and manner on this day? What might he expect to hear from her?

Objective 2(6.12)(J) – *The student is expected to recognize and interpret literary devices such as flashback, foreshadowing, and symbolism.*

4 The reader can tell from this story that for the Inuit people of Arctic Bay, soapstone carving was —

F an enjoyable hobby

G a means of survival

H a beautiful, lost art

J a way to become famous

💡 **HINT**
Read the section that describes life in this Inuit village. How does producing artwork help the people?

Objective 4(6.10)(H) – *The student is expected to draw inferences such as conclusions or generalizations and support them with text evidence [and experience].*

Answers

1 Ⓐ Ⓑ Ⓒ Ⓓ	2 Ⓕ Ⓖ Ⓗ Ⓙ	3 Ⓐ Ⓑ Ⓒ Ⓓ	4 Ⓕ Ⓖ Ⓗ Ⓙ

GO ➡

5 Why did Aola decide to learn soapstone carving?

A He admired the beautiful artwork.

B His grandmother believed he had a special talent for the art.

C He hoped to impress his grandmother by becoming an artist.

D He knew his family was in trouble because his father had lost his job.

💡 **HINT**
Read paragraph 8. What has Aola just been told.

Objective 2(6.12)(F) – The student is expected to analyze characters, including their traits, motivations, conflicts, points of view, relationships, and changes they undergo.

6 Which excerpt from the story best shows that Grandmother thinks Aola is ready to learn to carve?

F *Today, Aola's grandmother seemed weary, and her expression was brooding and tense.*

G *Aola understood the significance of her words. There would be less money for clothing, food, and other necessities.*

H *His grandmother looked up at him, unprepared for his comment.*

J *To his surprise, the elderly woman did not argue with him. Instead, she began talking to him in a way that was unfamiliar.*

💡 **HINT**
Find the part of the story where Aola says he is ready to carve. When does his grandmother seem willing to teach him?

Objective 4(6.10)(H) – The student is expected to draw inferences such as conclusions or generalizations and support them with text evidence [and experience].

7 Look at this web, which shows some ideas from the story.

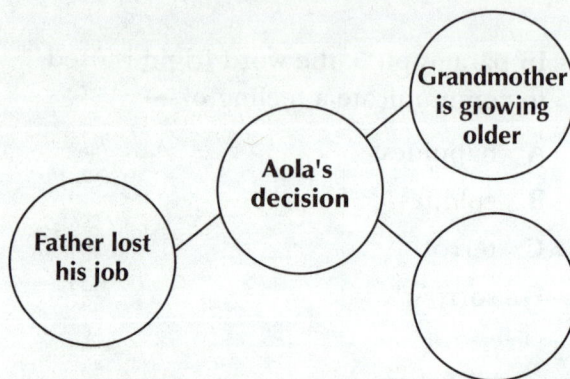

Which idea belongs in the empty oval?

A Aola's desire for spring

B Aola's love of fishing and trapping

C Carving is a valuable skill

D Grandmother carves well

💡 **HINT**
Which best fits the web's main idea?

Objective 3(6.10)(L) – The student is expected to represent text information in different ways such as in outline, timeline, or graphic organizer.

8 Why did Grandmother realize that Aola was ready to learn the art of carving?

F He was almost thirteen years old and seemed mature for his age.

G He understood the shape and possibilities of his stone.

H He handled the carving tools well.

J He could earn a lot of money.

💡 **HINT**
Look for an action that pleases Grandmother towards the end of the story.

Objective 2(6.12)(F) – The student is expected to analyze characters, including their traits, motivations, conflicts, points of view, relationships, and changes they undergo.

Answers

5 Ⓐ Ⓑ Ⓒ Ⓓ 6 Ⓕ Ⓖ Ⓗ Ⓙ 7 Ⓐ Ⓑ Ⓒ Ⓓ 8 Ⓕ Ⓖ Ⓗ Ⓙ **GO▶**

22

DIRECTIONS: Carefully read the selection. Then answer the questions.

Horace Pippin: An American Folk Artist

1   The American folk artist Horace Pippin was born in Pennsylvania in 1888. He was introduced to art in an unusual way. An African American, he served in the military during World War I. Pippin spent months in deep ditches called trenches. Here he began to sketch scenes of battle. While in France, Pippin was hit by a German soldier's bullet. The bullet was a special one that exploded when it hit him. It shattered his right shoulder. Doctors attached his shoulder to his upper arm, using a steel plate.

Horace Pippin (shown at right) receiving an award

2   Pippin was discharged from the army in 1919. The urge to draw was still with him, but his handicapped right arm made it almost impossible. Pippin did not lose hope, however. He invented a way to draw that involved using a hot poker to burn grooves in wood. He propped the poker between his right arm and his knee and used his left hand to guide the wood. Pippin sketched images into the wood and later painted within the grooves. This was a painstaking method of creating art, but he was determined to work again. Slowly, Pippin's right arm grew stronger. At last, he was able to paint with brushes on canvas.

3   Pippin usually made a sketch of his subject before he painted it. He made most of his paintings small because he still suffered pain in his right arm. He used any paint he could find, including house paint. Pippin worked this way for twelve years. In 1937, his paintings were discovered during a showing at the Art Association Annual Invitational in West Chester County, Pennsylvania. The next year, four of his works were displayed in the Museum of Modern Art show, *Masters of Popular Painting*. Critics called him a <u>primitive</u> painter in the style of Grandma Moses and Henri Rousseau. These painters were untrained and created original, fresh, and bold art. Pippin's work was dramatic, but he did not have a formal technique. His reputation grew after Dr. Albert Barnes, an art collector from Philadelphia, saw an exhibition of his paintings at the Carlen Gallery in that city. Robert Carlen had also been

GO

My notes about what I am reading ✏️

showing the work of another folk artist, Edward Hicks. In 1947, the critic Selden Rodman published the first book on the work of Horace Pippin. Now Pippin was known throughout America to those who loved native art.

4   Horace Pippin was a Northerner who only made one visit to the South, yet many of his finest paintings have Southern themes. One powerful picture, *The Whipping* (1941), depicts the manager of a plantation beating a slave. Another work, *Zachariah* (1943), shows an elderly black man supporting a poor, wounded white man somewhere in the woods at sunset. The subject suggests a slave helping an injured soldier, although the artist never commented on the meaning of the picture. Pippin also did a series of paintings of Abraham Lincoln and John Brown. Both of these men spoke out and took action against slavery. Pippin's works share the theme of freedom from slavery. It is interesting that Pippin made only a few pictures about the cruel treatment of slaves. He was more interested in recreating a world where people lived simply and nobly. His subjects are often heroes. Some, like Abraham Lincoln, were famous, but most were everyday people.

5   Pippin once told an interviewer something interesting about the way he worked. He said that before he touched paper or canvas, he created a whole picture in his mind. He kept the images in his head until he decided whether the subject was worth painting. By the time he was ready to pick up his brush, he could "see" all the forms and details clearly. He worked with tiny brush strokes, guiding his right hand with his left. This gave him enough pressure to make strong lines and forms.

6   Horace Pippin died in 1946, just after the end of World War II. Today, there is still much interest in his work. His originality and themes have won him a place among the best folk artists of the United States.

Horace Pippin's Zachariah *(1943)*

GO ➤

Use "Horace Pippin: An American Folk Artist" (pp. 23–24) to answer questions 9–15.

9 Why did Pippin keep an image in his head for a while before he painted it?

A He wanted to research the subject.

B He wanted to consider whether or not the subject was worth painting.

C He wanted to find the right materials to recreate the subject.

D He wanted to consider whether others would like the subject.

HINT
The answer is directly in the article. Find and reread the part that discusses the topic of the question.

Objective 3(6.10)(E) – *The student is expected to use the text's structure or progression of ideas such as cause and effect or chronology to locate and recall information.*

10 How is paragraph 3 organized?

F It describes Pippin's work and then explains how it was discovered.

G It discusses the development of American folklore art.

H It compares the work of Grandma Moses to that of Horace Pippin.

J It describes step-by-step how Pippin created a painting.

HINT
What topics are discussed in paragraph 3? How are the topics developed?

Objective 4(6.12)(I) – *The student is expected to analyze ways authors organize and present ideas such as through cause/effect, compare/contrast, inductively, deductively, or chronologically.*

11 Why did Pippin work on small canvases?

A He did not want to worsen the pain from his wounded arm.

B He believed that his subjects were best depicted in small pictures.

C He did not have enough money to buy large quantities of canvas.

D He wanted to paint small subjects.

HINT
Reread paragraph 3 of the article.

Objective 3(6.10)(E) – *The student is expected to use the text's structure or progression of ideas such as cause and effect or chronology to locate and recall information.*

12 Look at this portion of an outline below.

> **A. Early Work and Influences**
>   **1. Pippin sketches battle scenes while on the front lines.**
>   2. _____

Which best fits in the blank?

F Pippin works with short brush strokes and small canvases.

G Wounded in battle, Pippin must relearn how to draw and paint.

H Art critics compare Pippin's works to those of other folklore artists.

J Pippin gains fame for his paintings.

HINT
Which choice best supports the main idea "Early Work and Influences"?

Objective 3(6.10)(L) – *The student is expected to represent text information in different ways such as in outline, timeline, or graphic organizer.*

Answers

| 9 Ⓐ Ⓑ Ⓒ Ⓓ | 10 Ⓕ Ⓖ Ⓗ Ⓙ | 11 Ⓐ Ⓑ Ⓒ Ⓓ | 12 Ⓕ Ⓖ Ⓗ Ⓙ |

GO ➡

13 Which of the following is the best summary of the article?

A Horace Pippin was a soldier during World War I. A German shot him, and shattered his right shoulder. Later, he had surgery that allowed him to use his right arm. He had to relearn how to draw and paint, but eventually he found a good way to express his ideas through art.

B Horace Pippin's desire to create art was threatened by a serious battle wound. He overcame his physical handicap and had a successful career as an artist. An American primitive, Pippin is often compared to the painters Edward Hicks and Grandma Moses. His paintings are appreciated today as fine examples of American folklore art.

C Horace Pippin was an American painter who lived from 1888 to 1946. Pippin has been compared to other American primitive artists. He is the subject of a book by Selden Rodman.

D Horace Pippin's wounded arm troubled him for much of his life. He had to develop a new style because of his handicap. Pippin worked on small canvases and used short brushstrokes. He often imagined what a finished painting would look like before setting brush to canvas. Pippin's work is thought of as original and fresh.

HINT
A good summary contains most of the key points of a selection. Which choice includes the main ideas from the article?

Objective 1(6.10)(G) – *The student is expected to paraphrase and summarize text to recall, inform, or organize ideas.*

14 The most likely reason the author wrote this article was to —

F explain how Horace Pippin survived a serious war injury

G persuade readers to view a collection of Pippin's artworks

H describe the career of Horace Pippin, an American painter

J discuss the contribution of African American artists to modern art

HINT
Some of the answer choices are too narrow, while another is too general.

Objective 3(6.12)(A) – *The student is expected to identify the purposes of different types of texts such as to inform, influence, express, or entertain.*

15 Read the dictionary entry below for the word primitive.

primitive \ prim´i tiv \ *adj* **1.** ancient **2.** relating to the earlier stages of human development **3.** not valuable **4.** basic; not taught

In paragraph 3, the meaning of the word primitive is most like which of the following definitions?

A Definition 1   **C** Definition 3
B Definition 2   **D** Definition 4

HINT
Which definition best fits the meaning of the sentence? Are there any answer choices that you can rule out?

Objective 1(6.9)(B) – *The student is expected to draw on experiences to bring meanings to words in context such as interpreting [idioms,] multiple-meaning words, and analogies.*

Answers

| 13 Ⓐ Ⓑ Ⓒ Ⓓ | 14 Ⓕ Ⓖ Ⓗ Ⓙ | 15 Ⓐ Ⓑ Ⓒ Ⓓ | GO➤ |

DIRECTIONS: Carefully read the selection. Then answer the questions.

Fiesta

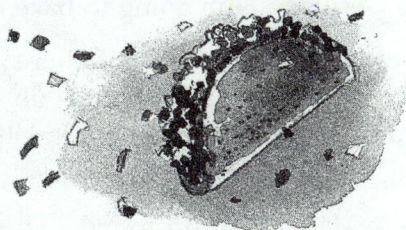

My notes about what I am reading

When Ms. Shapiro asked her sixth-grade class to share something special about their families, Luz was puzzled. "There *is* nothing special about my family. My sister goes to this school, my father is a cook in a Mexican restaurant, and my mother works in an office downtown."

"Why not share one of your dad's recipes with the class?" Ms. Shapiro suggested. "After all, everyone loves to eat! And Mexican food is extremely popular in our <u>region</u>, as I'm sure you know."

Luz's face brightened. "Customers say my father makes the best tacos this side of the border. I'll bring some in this week."

"Please write down the recipe, too," the teacher said. "That way, we can all do some experimenting in our own kitchens."

All week, Ms. Shapiro's students were busy bringing in stories, objects, and even pets from home. Indira Singh showed the girls the correct way to drape a sari so that the simple piece of cloth became an elegant outfit. Liz Green toted her African Grey parrot, who delighted the class by singing "Yankee Doodle Dandy." Spiro Kazantakis brought in the journal his great-grandfather had kept when he was a soldier in World War II. The journal made thrilling reading. Dennis McCallum displayed a photograph of a castle in the Scottish highlands. When students asked why the picture was special, he explained that his McCallum ancestors had occupied the castle for three centuries. "Now it is a public museum. I took a tour through the place last summer. It was incredible—suits of armor, old kilts, rusty swords—the whole works!"

By Thursday, nearly everyone had made a presentation. Only Luz and Lucia Alboni were left. "Tomorrow, class, we are going to have a real *fiesta*. Luz is bringing her father's delicious tacos, and Lucia is going to demonstrate an Italian dance called the *tarantella*. We'll have music and a main course—would anyone like to volunteer to bring in drinks and dessert?"

Keisha Jackson appointed herself food coordinator and quickly organized a list of food providers. There was a holiday mood in the classroom that lasted until the bell rang at three o'clock.

"Don't forget the lemonade and iced tea," Keisha reminded the volunteers as they filed out the door.

GO➡

"And I'm bringing a Bundt cake," Kathy Reiter reminded her. That's a special cake from Germany. "I'm going to bake it tonight."

At six o'clock the next morning, Luz and her father stood in the kitchen. Mr. Diego laid out the ingredients on the countertop. "Do you want to peel and chop the onions and garlic? Or will that make you cry?" he teased his older daughter.

"No, that only happens to Maria," Luz protested. "I never cry over onions—only spelling words."

Side by side, the two cooks chopped, sautéed, and simmered their ingredients until the kitchen was fragrant with spices and tender beef. When Maria staggered into the kitchen at seven o'clock looking for cereal and fruit, she sniffed the air, her black eyes widening. "We're having tacos for breakfast, Papa?"

"No, Luz is bringing them to school. You can have cereal at the dining-room table. How's that for fancy?" He quickly fixed the little girl a breakfast tray and got back to the taco assembly line.

When they were all finished spooning the meat mixture into the taco shells, Luz wrapped them carefully in aluminum foil. "I'll put them in the microwave before lunchtime. Mrs. Ramirez runs the cafeteria, and she said that would be okay."

"Let's make ourselves some toast and wash the pots and pans before your mother tries to brew her morning coffee." They cleaned up quickly. Luz had to run to the school bus with a shopping bag of tacos in one hand and a half-eaten piece of toast in the other.

The morning flew by; Ms. Shapiro got the spelling quiz over with

GO ➡

by ten o'clock and asked the students to start setting up for the *fiesta.* Some had brought decorations for the room, while others had brought extra refreshments. The teacher's desk became a serving table upon which the Diego family's tacos took their place.

"These tacos are absolutely wonderful!" exclaimed Reesa Willard.

"Did you remember to bring in your recipe?" Ms. Shapiro asked.

"Yes, I'll post it on the classroom bulletin board," Luz promised.

My notes about what I am reading

My Dad's Authentic Mexican Tacos

- 4 pounds of beef chuck or pot roast, salted and peppered to taste
- 1/3 cup of olive oil
- 1 cup of water
- 2 cloves of crushed or finely chopped garlic
- 1 large onion, peeled and sliced
- 1 green bell pepper
- 1 cup of tomato sauce
- 1 teaspoon of salt
- 1 bay leaf
- 1 teaspoon of chili powder
- 1/2 teaspoon of cumin (optional)

After you rub the salt and pepper into the meat, you should heat a large frying pan on the stovetop. Add a little olive oil to the pan. Brown the meat, stirring frequently so that it is evenly cooked. Cover the pan and simmer on a low heat for about two hours. Add a cup of water to the meat so that it doesn't dry out.

When the meat is cooked, let it cool with the cover of the pan in place. Then shred the meat and remove any bones. Put the meat in a bowl along with the juices from the pan.

Heat the pan again and add the leftover oil. Sauté the garlic and onions, then add the green pepper and allow the vegetables to cook for a few more minutes. Add the remaining ingredients along with the shredded meat and juice. Cover the pan and simmer the mixture for another 15 or 20 minutes. Now you are ready to fill a warm wheat tortilla. If you want a topping, you can use salsa, sour cream, shredded lettuce, and/or chopped scallions.

GO

> **Use "Fiesta" (pp. 27–29) to answer questions 16–23.**

16 When Ms. Shapiro gave the students their assignment, Luz was puzzled because —

F Ms. Shapiro did not usually ask students to share personal experiences with one another

G Luz did not understand what was being asked of her

H Ms. Shapiro did not clearly explain what the students were to do

J Luz did not believe she would have anything of value to share with the class

HINT
Read the first paragraph. How does Luz feel about her family's daily life?

Objective 1(6.10)(F) – *The student is expected to determine a text's main (or major) ideas and how those ideas are supported with details.*

17 In the second paragraph, the word <u>region</u> means —

A block

B country

C area

D street

HINT
The best answer choice is suggested by the overall context of the second paragraph.

Objective 1(6.9)(B) – *The student is expected to draw on experiences to bring meanings to words in context such as interpreting [idioms,] multiple-meaning words, and analogies.*

18 Which sentence from the story best shows that Luz was in a hurry Friday morning?

F *At six o'clock the next morning, Luz and her father stood in the kitchen.*

G *"I'll put them in the microwave before lunch time."*

H *They cleaned up quickly.*

J *Luz had to run to the school bus with a shopping bag in one hand and a half-eaten piece of toast in the other.*

HINT
Which answer choice indicates Luz doing something fast, as if in a hurry?

Objective 4(6.10)(H) – *The student is expected to draw inferences such as conclusions or generalizations and support them with text evidence [and experience].*

19 What does Luz mean when she says that her "father makes the best tacos this side of the border"?

A That her father's tacos are better than those made in Mexico

B That the chefs of Mexico are more skilled than her father

C That her father makes the best tacos in the United States

D That her father's tacos are the best in town

HINT
What border is Luz referring to? Why would she compare the food in two different countries?

Objective 2(6.12)(F) – *The student is expected to analyze characters, including their traits, motivations, conflicts, points of view, relationships, and changes they undergo.*

Answers

| 16 Ⓕ Ⓖ Ⓗ Ⓙ | 17 Ⓐ Ⓑ Ⓒ Ⓓ | 18 Ⓕ Ⓖ Ⓗ Ⓙ | 19 Ⓐ Ⓑ Ⓒ Ⓓ |

GO➤

20 From what the reader learns about Luz, which statement would not be reasonable?

F Luz has a close relationship with her father.

G Luz does not feel proud of her Mexican heritage.

H Luz enjoys cooking special meals at home.

J At first, Luz does not think her family is special.

HINT
Use the information in the selection to choose the best answer to the question. You can rule out three answers because each of them is true.

Objective 2(6.12)(F) – *The student is expected to analyze characters, including their traits, motivations, conflicts, points of view, relationships, and changes they undergo.*

21 Why does the author include the recipe for tacos?

A To prove that tacos are easy to make

B To compare tacos to other recipes using meat

C To present Luz as a realistic character in the story

D To show readers how to make tacos, a favorite Mexican meal

HINT
Sometimes a selection can include more than one type of writing. This selection is a combination of narrative and informative writing. Consider the author's purpose for providing a complete recipe.

Objective 3(6.12)(A) – *The student is expected to identify the purposes of different types of texts such as to inform, influence, express, or entertain.*

22 Look at the flow chart below, which shows the order of some of the steps for preparing the tacos.

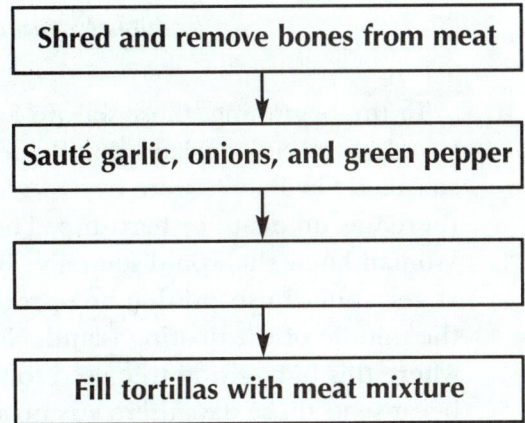

| Shred and remove bones from meat |
| Sauté garlic, onions, and green pepper |
| |
| Fill tortillas with meat mixture |

Which step belongs in the empty box?

F Add a little olive oil to the pan

G Reheat pan to cook the onions

H Add remaining ingredients

J Add a cup of water to the meat

HINT
Note the order of the steps in the recipe.

Objective 3(6.10)(L) – *The student is expected to represent text information in different ways such as in outline, timeline, or graphic organizer.*

23 According to the recipe, which ingredient is not necessary?

A Cumin   **C** Garlic

B Salt   **D** Onion

HINT
One item is followed by a word that indicates the cook has a choice to include it.

Objective 3(6.10)(E) – *The student is expected to use the text's structure or progression of ideas such as cause and effect or chronology to locate and recall information.*

Answers

| 20 Ⓕ Ⓖ Ⓗ Ⓙ | 21 Ⓐ Ⓑ Ⓒ Ⓓ | 22 Ⓕ Ⓖ Ⓗ Ⓙ | 23 Ⓐ Ⓑ Ⓒ Ⓓ |

GO

31

DIRECTIONS: Carefully read the two selections. Then answer the questions.

Sky Woman and the Earth

an Iroquois Creation Myth

1   In the beginning, there was no Earth as we know it, and the people lived on an island that floated high in the sky. These so-called Sky People were free of regret and sorrow because there was no death or hardship. Then the day came when Sky Woman knew she would soon give birth to twins. This so angered her husband that he uprooted the Tree of Light in the middle of the floating island. Now, there was a big hole where this light-giving tree used to stand. It began to grow dark because in those days there was no sun. Sky Woman tried to see what was in the hole. As she leaned over to get a look at the waters that covered the earth, her enraged husband shoved her. Sky Woman found herself falling through the hole into the water.

2   Two birds took pity on Sky Woman. They caught her in midair and bore her on their backs to the water animals that lived below the island. Knowing Sky Woman could only live on land, the water animals tried to gather mud from the ocean floor, but the task was too hard. Only Little Toad was able to fill his mouth with mud. The animals spread this mud on the back of Big Turtle, and the mud grew until it formed the land of North America. Here Sky Woman lived, and here she gave birth to twin boys, whom she named Flint and Sapling. Flint was cold and hard, but Sapling was tender and kind.

GO ➤

My notes about
what I am
reading

3   As the two boys grew up, they each adopted the work of creation. Sapling made rivers full of fish that had no bones so that the people could easily eat them. He made plants that were good to eat and friendly animals that helped people to survive. But Flint always tried to undo Sapling's work. He added bones to the fish and created monsters that Sapling exiled to the place beneath the earth. He created winter so that the people would suffer cold and hunger.

4   At last, Flint and Sapling began to fight. They fought and fought until Sapling finally overcame his brother. But gods do not die. Flint still lives on the back of Big Turtle; and when he is very angry, the earth belches lava and fire.

Sun Mother

an Australian Aborigine Creation Myth

1   Long ago, the spirits of the earth lay sleeping, all except the Father of All Spirits. One day he roused Sun Mother, telling her to awaken the sleeping spirits. Sun Mother began to walk all over the world. Wherever she went, plants began to grow. Seeing this, Sun Mother thought she had done well and took a well-deserved rest. The Father of All Spirits was pleased when he saw what she had done, but he knew she was not yet finished. "Your work is not done," he instructed her. "Go into the caves and wake up the spirits who are still asleep."

2   Sun Mother crawled into the caves, trailing her bright light. Winged insects awoke and flew out of the caves. They soon were buzzing among the flowers in the fields. Sun Mother thought she had done well and took another well-deserved rest, but the Father of All Spirits told her, "Your work is not done. Go and rouse the rest of the spirits."

3   This time, Sun Mother found the deepest cave and brought her light to its frozen tunnels. The heat of her body melted the ice, creating rivers and streams. Next she made frogs, lizards, fish, and snakes. Finally, she called forth the spirits of the birds, who arose in their many-colored splendor. Sun Mother told these animals to enjoy the earth's bounty and live in harmony. The Father of All Spirits praised her work, and she was allowed to return to her home in the sky to rest. But when she vanished, leaving night behind her, the animals and the flowers thought she had abandoned them forever and were frozen with terror. They dared not move until she arose again in the East and spread her beams across the earth. At last they understood that she would come and go each day.

GO ▶

My notes about what I am reading ✎

4   All was well until the creatures began to quarrel. They were jealous of one another and unhappy. So Sun Mother allowed each animal to take a new form. However, she did not like all the new shapes her children had chosen, so she changed these again. She created some very odd animals, like the platypus, which had the parts of many different kinds of creatures. With its duck bill, big teeth, and beaver tail, the platypus was an odd thing to observe. Sun Mother did not know whether the Father of All Spirits would be pleased, so she gave birth to two children: Morning Star and Moon. Because Sun Mother had created them from her own being, she knew that they would always remain the same. Morning Star and Moon came down to Earth and were the first ancestors of the people.

GO ▶

Use "Sky Woman and the Earth" (pp. 32–33) to answer questions 24–27.

24 According to the story, North America was created from —

F a huge hole filled with water

G the body of Sky Woman

H mud from the bottom of the sea

J the Tree of Light

HINT
How did the animals create a solid piece of land where Sky Woman could live?

Objective 1(6.10)(F) – *The student is expected to determine a text's main (or major) ideas and how those ideas are supported with details.*

25 In paragraph 1, the author writes that the "Sky People were free of regret and sorrow" to show that they —

A had overcome great hardships in the past

B lived happy, carefree lives and were at peace

C were soon to encounter trouble in their world

D received regret and sorrow free of charge

HINT
Think about the Sky People before Sky Woman's husband became angry. What were their lives like?

Objective 2(6.12)(J) – *The student is expected to recognize and interpret literary devices such as flashback, foreshadowing, and symbolism.*

26 Most of the events in the story were supposed to have taken place —

F In North America

G on a floating island in the sky

H under the surface of the ocean

J in an imaginary country

HINT
What is the myth's setting? Which details from the story give this information?

Objective 2(6.12)(G) – *The student is expected to recognize and analyze story plot, setting, and problem resolution.*

27 Which excerpt from the story is the best example of the value of nature?

A *As the two boys grew up, they each adopted the work of creation.*

B *He made plants that were good to eat and friendly animals that helped people to survive.*

C *He added bones to the fish and created monsters that Sapling exiled to the place beneath the earth.*

D *Flint still lives on the back of Big Turtle; and when he is very angry, the earth belches lava and fire.*

HINT
Think about what the word "nature" means. Which choice best describes the importance of nature?

Objective 4(6.10)(H) – *The student is expected to draw inferences such as conclusions or generalizations and support them with text evidence.*

Answers

| 24 Ⓕ Ⓖ Ⓗ Ⓙ | 25 Ⓐ Ⓑ Ⓒ Ⓓ | 26 Ⓕ Ⓖ Ⓗ Ⓙ | 27 Ⓐ Ⓑ Ⓒ Ⓓ |

GO

> **Use "Sun Mother" (pp. 33–34) to answer questions 28–29.**

28 The tone of the story can be described as—

F tranquil   H exciting

G joyful   J sad

💡 **HINT**
The *tone* is the mood of the selection. It represents the overall attitude of the author. What is the language of the story like? How would the author sound reading it aloud?

Objective 4(6.12)(K) – The student is expected to recognize how style, tone, and mood contribute to the effect of the text.

29 Why did the animals quarrel?

A None of the animals wanted to share the earth with the others.

B Sun Mother paid more attention to some animals than to others.

C Each was jealous of the others and wished to look different.

D All of the animals wanted to look like Morning Star and Moon.

💡 **HINT**
Reread the last paragraph. Why were the animals unhappy?

Objective 3(6.10)(E) – The student is expected to use the text's structure or progression of ideas such as cause and effect or chronology to locate and recall information.

> **Use "Sky Woman and the Earth" and "Sun Mother" to answer question 30.**

30 Look at the diagram below, which shows information from both selections.

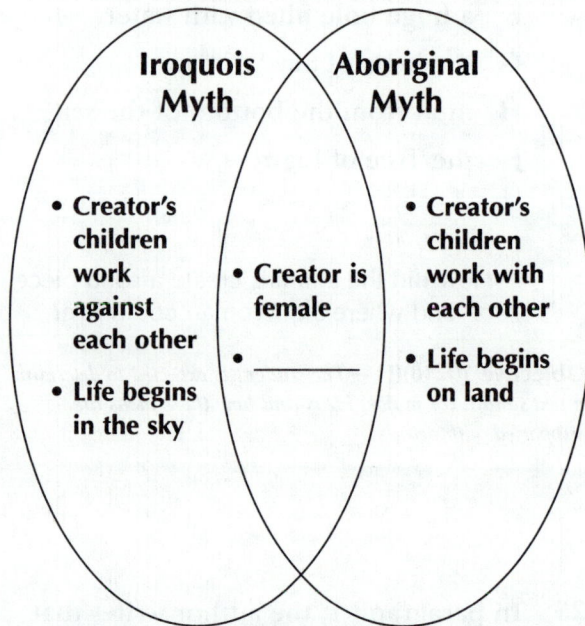

Iroquois Myth

- Creator's children work against each other
- Life begins in the sky

- Creator is female
- _____

Aboriginal Myth

- Creator's children work with each other
- Life begins on land

Which statement belongs in the blank?

F Creator bears twins

G Animals quarrel

H Setting is an island

J Creator brings light

💡 **HINT**
To belong in the center of the diagram, the statement must be true of both selections. Scan the stories to check the accuracy of each answer choice.

Objective 3(6.12)(C) – The student is expected to compare communication in different forms such as [contrasting a dramatic performance with a print version of the same story or] comparing story variants.

Answers

| 28 Ⓕ Ⓖ Ⓗ Ⓙ | 29 Ⓐ Ⓑ Ⓒ Ⓓ | 30 Ⓕ Ⓖ Ⓗ Ⓙ |

STOP

Writing

DIRECTIONS: Read the introduction below. Then read the passage. Answer the questions that follow. Fill in the correct answers at the bottom of the page.

PART I: Revising and Editing

Junius wrote a paper to describe the life and works of a twentieth century hero. He has asked you to help him revise and edit it. After you read the paper, think about the suggestions you could give Junius for correcting and improving it. Then answer the questions that follow.

Mohandas Gandhi: India's Champion

(1) Many people have fought to gain freedom, but few have used peaceful means for the same end. (2) Mohandas K. Gandhi, India great leader, freed his country from British rule without aiming a gun or raising a sword. (3) This great man was small and thin but had the strength of his beliefs. (4) His program of Satyagraha involved civil disobedience. (5) This included taking part in strikes and demonstrations without the use of violence.

(6) Young Gandhi began his life as many other people of his time and place did. (7) He married at age thirteen and had four children. (8) He studied to be a lawyer, not a politikal leader. (9) Then a business trip to South Africa showed him how unfairly his people were treated. (10) Gandhi stayed in Africa for twenty-one years working to improve the lives of Indians there.

(11) Back home in India again, Gandhi took part in the movement to end British rule. (12) When riots erupted, Gandhi fasted for peace. (13) They also started a program of hand spinning and weaving cloth. (14) This gave Indians work and self-respect. (15) It was a way to show the British that they no longer needed their cloth goods.

GO

(16) India was granted its freedom, India and Pakistan became two warring countries. (17) This was a tragedy to Gandhi because he had worked for years to teach people to get along with each other. (18) In 1948, when Gandhi was seventy-eight years old, he was assassinated by an angry Hindu. (19) He left behind many followers. (20) Writing a book about his life titled *My Experiments with Truth.*

GO ➤

1   What change, if any, should be made in sentence 2?

A   Change *India* to **India's**

B   Change *freed* to **was freeing**

C   Change *raising* to **raised**

D   Make no change

HINT
Check that punctuation is used correctly for possessive nouns. Are the verb tenses correct in the sentence?

Objective 6(7.16)(B) – *The student is expected to capitalize and punctuate correctly to clarify and enhance meaning such as capitalizing titles, using hyphens, semicolons, colons, possessives, and sentence punctuation.*

2   What change should be made in sentence 8?

F   Change *studied* to **has studied**

G   Change *lawyer* to **lawer**

H   Delete the comma after *lawyer*

J   Change *politikal* to **political**

HINT
You may use a dictionary to check the spelling of words that seem incorrect to you. Make sure the correct verb tense and punctuation is used.

Objective 6(7.16)(F) – *The student is expected to spell accurately in final drafts.*

3   What change, if any, should be made in sentence 10?

A   Add a comma after *years*

B   Change *years* to **year's**

C   Change *Indians* to **indians**

D   Make no change

HINT
Commas are used to set off phrases and clauses. Check to see if a possessive noun is in the sentence. Is capitalization correct throughout?

Objective 6(7.18)(H) – *The student is expected to proofread his/her own writing and that of others.*

4   Which transition word or phrase should be added to the beginning of sentence 15?

F   However,

G   For example,

H   Additionally,

J   But,

HINT
How does sentence 15 relate to the sentences before it? Which answer choice best reflects this relationship?

Objective 4(7.17)(B) – *The student is expected to use conjunctions to connect ideas meaningfully.*

Answers

| 1 Ⓐ Ⓑ Ⓒ Ⓓ | 2 Ⓕ Ⓖ Ⓗ Ⓙ | 3 Ⓐ Ⓑ Ⓒ Ⓓ | 4 Ⓕ Ⓖ Ⓗ Ⓙ |

GO➤

5 Which sentence could be added after sentence 15 to support the ideas in the third paragraph (sentences 11–15)?

A Altogether, Gandhi spent seven years in jail for political reasons.

B Gandhi's wife was a firm supporter of his views.

C There was tension between Hindus and Muslims for many years.

D Indians needed to believe that they could succeed as an independent nation.

HINT
Which sentence seems best to summarize the other sentences in the paragraph? Only one answer choice fits this question.

Objective 3(7.18)(C) – *The student is expected to revise selected drafts by adding, elaborating, deleting, combining, and rearranging text.*

6 Which of the following is the BEST way to rewrite the ideas in sentence 16?

F Since India was granted its freedom, India and Pakistan became two warring countries.

G India was granted its freedom and India and Pakistan became two warring countries.

H After India was granted its freedom, India and Pakistan became two warring countries.

J No revision is needed.

HINT
Which answer choice contains a word that shows the proper time sequence?

Objective 4(7.17)(B) – *The student is expected to use conjunctions to connect ideas meaningfully.*

7 What change, if any, should be made in sentence 18?

A Delete the comma after *1948*

B Change *was assassinated* to **had been assassinated**

C Change *Hindu* to **hindu**

D Make no change

HINT
Read the sentence carefully to determine whether there are any errors in grammar, spelling, or punctuation.

Objective 6(7.18)(H) – *The student is expected to proofread his/her own writing and that of others.*

8 Which of the following is NOT a complete sentence?

F Sentence 17

G Sentence 18

H Sentence 19

J Sentence 20

HINT
A complete sentence must have a subject and a verb. One of these choices does not.

Objective 4(7.17)(A) – *The student is expected to write in complete sentences, varying the types such as compound and complex sentences, and use appropriately punctuated independent and dependent clauses.*

Answers

5 Ⓐ Ⓑ Ⓒ Ⓓ	6 Ⓕ Ⓖ Ⓗ Ⓙ	7 Ⓐ Ⓑ Ⓒ Ⓓ	8 Ⓕ Ⓖ Ⓗ Ⓙ

STOP

PART II: Written Composition

> **Write a composition about why it is important to build relationships with people in your community.**

HINT
Think of some friends who live near you. What do you do with them? How do they make you feel? Why is it good to be friends with people in your community?

Objectives 1 and 2/All Expectations

• • •

First, do some prewriting on the following pages. Graphic organizers such as outlines, sequence maps, main idea maps, and compare-contrast grids can help you collect and organize your ideas. Organize your composition and decide how you want to write it. Then write your composition on the following two pages.

• • •

The information below will remind you of what to think about when you are writing your composition.

DON'T FORGET TO:

☐ write about why it is important to build lasting friendships with others

☐ write an essay that will hold your reader's interest

☐ make sure that each sentence you write adds to your reader's understanding of your ideas

☐ express your ideas in a clear, direct way

☐ include appropriate details to help your reader fully understand your topic and purpose for writing

☐ proofread your work for correct spelling, capitalization, punctuation, grammar, and sentences

GO

SPACE FOR PREWRITING

SPACE FOR PREWRITING

45

STOP

Now you will take two practice tests.

First you will take a practice test for the TAKS in Reading. Then you will take a practice test for the TAKS in Writing. Use the skills and hints you learned in the first section of this book to help you succeed on these tests.

Try using the following strategies as you take the two practice tests:

- ☐ Pay careful attention to directions.

- ☐ Read the entire question and all of the choices.

- ☐ Determine clearly what is being asked.

- ☐ Narrow down possible answers by getting rid of incorrect choices.

- ☐ Sometimes more than one answer may seem correct—choose the best answer.

- ☐ Be sure to mark answers in the appropriate place on your answer sheet.

- ☐ Do not spend too much time on any one question.

- ☐ Mark items to return to if time permits.

- ☐ Use any time remaining to review answers.

Also try using the following strategies as you write your composition:

- ☐ Plan what you want to say before you begin writing.

- ☐ Write your composition neatly on the lines within the box.

- ☐ Write as neatly and legibly as possible.

- ☐ Be sure to answer all parts of the question.

- ☐ Revise and edit your work.

- ☐ Use any time remaining to review your writing.

Sometimes people get nervous when they take a test. Try to remember what you have learned about taking tests. Knowing what to expect should help you feel more confident and improve your score.

Remember to use the separate answer sheet on page 141 to fill in your answers.

Reading

DIRECTIONS: Carefully read the selection. Then answer the questions.

In 1814, during the War of 1812 between Britain and America, British troops set fire to the White House and the Capitol. James Madison was the President during this war, which firmly established the United States as an independent nation. The following letter was written by a servant of Dolley Madison, the First Lady. Lucinda Martin is a fictional character, but someone very much like her must have existed and helped the President's wife.

Daring Dolley

My notes about what I am reading

August 22, 1840

Dear Mariana,

1   In your letter, you asked me to describe Mrs. James Madison. I am very happy to transcribe my memories of this remarkable woman. Nothing could describe her better than what occurred just before the burning of the White House, more than twenty-five years ago.

2   I was packing up the trunks that Wednesday, the twenty-third day of August. We were nearly alone in the White House, the President being away; he had joined General Winder after asking my mistress whether she had the courage to remain at home. Naturally, that brave soul said she only feared for him. The First Lady had no way of knowing that the Battle of Bladensburg would that day leave the city of Washington vulnerable to the enemy. Oh, she knew the troops were approaching, but not how soon they would march into sight. And I, of course, had no idea that there would be such little time for our trunks. There I was, putting away the precious things, the silver candlesticks and lovely dresses Mrs. Madison wore for parties. How little we realized what was about to befall us! I am an old woman now, but that terrible day taught me a lesson about what is valuable in this world.

3   The hour arrived when Mrs. Madison, my mistress, called out to me to hurry. "Don't trouble yourself about clothing and

GO

My notes about
what I am
reading

silver, Lucinda! The British will be here in a few hours."

4   "Oh, can't our troops stop them? Will they get right up to our doors?"

5   I was flustered, but my mistress was calm and collected. "I hope not, Lucinda. But if they should come, we must be prepared."

6   "What should I do, then?" I asked. "How must I prepare?"

7   "You will help me pack the Cabinet papers. These are important documents and cannot be destroyed."

8   We began filling the trunks with as many papers as we could. "We will only have one carriage to transport us, along with the papers," Mrs. Madison told me. "We must just do our best, Lucinda, to save what is essential to the government."

9   I did not then see how she could bear to part with her personal things, but now I do. She had a wisdom that was not always visible, for she was so cheery and charming. I agree with those who say my mistress could not sketch prettily or play an instrument perfectly. Mrs. Madison was raised as a Quaker. Those good people believe in the inner light and shun fancy displays. But my lady was the most gracious and polite hostess who ever lived. No offense to her good husband, but people would have found the White House a much duller place without lovely Miss Dolley. Her Wednesday evening <u>receptions</u> were the delight of the whole city.

10   But this Wednesday was very different. I hope I will be forgiven for reading my mistress's letter to her sister, which she started in the morning and finished just before half-past three in the afternoon. Never will I forget the words she wrote:

11   *Wednesday Morning, twelve o'clock.—Since sunrise I have been turning my spy-glass in every direction, and watching with unwearied anxiety, hoping to discover the approach of my dear husband and his friends; but, alas! I can descry only groups of military, wandering in all directions, as if there was a lack of arms, or of spirit to fight for their own fireside.*

12   Miss Dolley surely never lacked that spirit. What she must have thought when she heard the complete tale of how our men had scattered in confusion as the British came upon them!

13   Late in the afternoon, we succeeded in getting one more wagon. Then I was allowed to fill it with silver and other items that belonged to the White House. But that is not what I chiefly remember of this day.

GO

My notes about what I am reading

14   "We will not leave the house, Lucinda, until we have secured the portrait of General Washington. That must not be destroyed, no matter what becomes of the remainder of the property," Miss Dolley announced. Mr. Carroll, a firm friend of the Madisons, came to tell my mistress to abandon the White House at once.

15   "You are in great danger if you remain another hour," he told her.

16   "So be it," the First Lady replied, throwing back her elegant head. She called for two male servants to remove the picture from its place. Finding that it was tightly screwed into the wall, she decided to waste no more time. She commanded the picture frame to be broken and the canvas to be removed.

17   Two gentlemen of the state of New York were present, so the President's lady entrusted the portrait to them. She thanked them for their help, saying that the portrait was part of our national heritage. The gentlemen replied that it was a great honor to be so trusted by none other than Mrs. Madison.

18   You probably know the rest of what happened at that awful time. Mrs. Madison joined her husband in safety, but the White House burned to the ground. The picture of Mr. Washington was the only valuable thing that survived the fire. The enemy burned down our Capitol building, too. Then fate came to our aid in the form of a rainstorm that extinguished the fire. Our city was safe. And I remember, too, that the First Lady thanked me for the small part I had played in assisting her.

Yours truly,

Great-aunt Lucinda

GO➤

Use "Daring Dolley" (pp. 47–49) to answer questions 1–9.

1 Why does the author include the introduction to the letter?

A To explain why Dolley Madison wanted to save the picture of Washington

B To describe life in an American city in the 1800's

C To establish that the story is based on an event of historical importance

D To present Lucinda Martin as the heroine of the story

2 In paragraph 9, the word <u>receptions</u> refers to —

F the act of receiving

G social gatherings

H radio or television signals

J the way in which a thing is accepted

3 The advantage of learning about this historical event from Lucinda's point of view is that it helps the reader understand why —

A the British were so determined to destroy the White House

B Lucinda Martin chose to obey her mistress's instructions

C the War of 1812 was an important event in United States history

D Dolley Madison's actions that day were daring and admirable

GO➤

4 The statement "How little we realized what was about to befall us!" is meant to —

F foreshadow a significant event that will be described later in the narrative

G refer to the passage of time since the burning of the White House took place

H compare the old White House with the White House that was later rebuilt

J flash back to the narrator's feelings at the time of these events

5 The tone of paragraph 2 can be described best as —

A desperate

B angry

C boastful

D solemn

6 Which of the following is the best summary of the letter?

F On the day that British troops marched toward the White House, Lucinda Martin was hurriedly packing expensive items. She was only allowed to pack one trunk of these because her mistress was more concerned with saving important documents. Lucinda was nervous, but the First Lady remained calm and reasonable.

G The War of 1812 established American independence from Great Britain. The British succeeded in destroying the White House and the Capitol, but the rest of the city was saved by a rainstorm. Some valuables were rescued from the White House, including the portrait of General Washington.

H When the British marched on Washington, D.C. during the War of 1812, the First Lady showed courage and decisiveness. She organized the staff in the preservation of valuables, especially the portrait of General Washington. Because of her actions, a national treasure was saved.

J Lucinda Martin was a faithful servant to Dolley Madison, the First Lady. She helped to organize the packing and removal of precious items from the White House just before it was burned to the ground by British troops. Lucinda would never forget that frightening day during the War of 1812.

GO →

7 Why was Dolley Madison so determined to save the portrait of General Washington?

A The painting of the first President symbolized American independence and national pride.

B Her husband, President Madison, had asked her to protect the portrait at all costs.

C Despite her Quaker upbringing, Dolley Madison greatly appreciated fine art.

D The painting was worth a great deal of money, and she did not want the British to have it.

8 Paragraph 9 is important to the story because it —

F shows what Quakers believe in

G reveals that President Madison had a colorless and dull personality

H describes the character and accomplishments of Dolley Madison

J discusses the social life of Washington, D.C., during President Madison's term of office

9 Look at this outline of events narrated in Lucinda Martin's letter.

> **A. The British Advance on Washington, D.C.**
>   1. **American troops scatter under fire from the British.**
>   2. **British troops are able to march into the capital.**
> **B. The White House Prepares for the Invasion**
>   1. **Mrs. Madison directs that important documents are packed.**
>   2. **Careful decisions about packing are made.**
> **C. Mrs. Madison's Decision**
>   1. **Mrs. Madison orders that General Washington's portrait be removed from its frame.**
>   2. _____

Which of these statements belongs in the blank under the heading "Mrs. Madison's Decision"?

A Mrs. Madison shows wisdom and the ability to plan carefully.

B The British set fire to the Capitol building, but the city is spared.

C A second wagon is secured for salvaging valuables from the White House.

D Mrs. Madison asks two gentlemen from New York to carry the portrait away and put it into safe-keeping.

GO➤

DIRECTIONS: Carefully read the two selections. Then answer the questions.

Abraham Lincoln and the Union

My notes about what I am reading

FROM OUR SPECIAL WAR CORRESPONDENT.
"City Point, Va., April —, 8.30 A.M.
"All seems well with us."—A. Lincoln.

1   The man who became our sixteenth President grew up on the frontier. He was born in 1809 in a log cabin. His pioneer family kept moving on in search of a better life. There was little opportunity for formal schooling, but Abraham Lincoln managed to learn. He borrowed books and studied between chores. Because he was bright and eager to learn, this country boy would become a lawyer, a politician, and finally, the President of the United States.

2   As a lawyer, Lincoln became well-known in the Illinois State Supreme and Federal courts. With his sharp mind and pleasant manner, Lincoln won the respect of all those he met. Through his work in the courts, he became interested in politics. Yet he was not passionate about any particular cause until slavery threatened to divide the nation.

3   In the 1850's, slavery was already in the eastern part of the United States. Some people wanted to extend slavery to the western territories. Democrat Stephen A. Douglas and his followers managed to change the terms of the Missouri Compromise. This act had prohibited slavery in the Louisiana Purchase. Now, the law would allow the people of Kansas and Nebraska to decide whether they wished to hold slaves. Lincoln was firmly against the spread of slavery. He spoke out against it so powerfully that the new Republican party urged him to run

GO➤

53

against Douglas for the presidency. To the surprise of many, he won the election.

My notes about what I am reading

4   Lincoln took office in February 1861. He faced many problems. Seven southern states had separated, or seceded, from the Union. Jefferson Davis had just become the first President of the Confederate States of America. Debates raged in Congress. The treasury contained almost no money. The army was weak and officers kept heading South to join the new Confederacy. Lincoln was almost unknown to the American people, so they did not trust him. He was sloppy with paperwork and not a very good administrator. He did not believe in controlling the men in his Cabinet, who frequently argued with one another.

5   Yet Lincoln had a power that changed the course of history. He was a persuasive speaker of great conviction. Furthermore, he would do almost anything to keep the Union together. As commander-in-chief of the United States Army, Lincoln organized his generals and raised money to keep the war going. There were serious setbacks on the battlefield. Some people lost faith in Lincoln and blamed him for the losses. The President grieved over the deaths of the soldiers, but he never gave up hope that the side of justice and right would win. Abraham Lincoln lived just long enough to see the North defeat the South in the Civil War.

Jefferson Davis and the Confederacy

1   Jefferson Davis was the first and last President of the Confederate States of America. He was born in 1808, one year after the birth of Abraham Lincoln. Like many young men from wealthy families, he went to a military academy. He served in the army until his marriage, when he became a cotton planter. He was drawn to politics and became known as a public speaker. Davis often spoke out in favor of keeping a strong Union. His change of heart was the stuff of history.

GO▶

My notes about
what I am
reading

2   During the war with Mexico, Davis served as colonel of the 1st Mississippi volunteers. He showed great courage, fighting on when severely wounded. In 1848 he was elected to the Senate. He later served in President Franklin Pierce's cabinet as U.S. Secretary of War. When Pierce left office in 1857, Davis once again became a state senator from Mississippi. He won the hearts of his fellow Southerners by warmly supporting the right of any state to make its own laws.

3   Davis's supporters wanted him to run for President in 1860. However, Davis said he did not seek the presidency. He continued to speak out for states' rights. As a planter, he had a reason to protect the slave system. Like many other Southerners, Davis did not want the federal government to get involved with slavery. He was called to Washington, D.C., to take part in a committee to study the country's problems. Yet Davis could not control what was happening in his home state. In January 1861, Mississippi left the Union. Other states would quickly follow.

4   In February 1861, Jefferson Davis became President of the Confederate States. He had given up his loyalty to the federal government. Now he was bound to the fate of the South. War broke out after an attack on Fort Sumter in South Carolina. The mood of Southerners was optimistic. Their men had been educated at military academies; the Northerners were known as a ragtag army. The planters felt that the war would be over in a few months. The South won the first few battles of the war, and Davis enjoyed great popularity as a leader.

5   With General Robert E. Lee as his strong arm, Davis felt certain of victory. But the Union Army proved stronger than expected. Davis had many disagreements with his officers, which weakened his position. The Civil War dragged on for four years, leaving the South in ruins. In April 1865, General Lee surrendered to the Northern commander, Ulysses S. Grant. Davis did not approve of the surrender, but the end had to come sometime. He was captured and put in prison for two years. After his release, Davis was again popular in the South. The ex-president went into private business, heading a life insurance company in Memphis, Tennessee.

GO➤

Use "Abraham Lincoln and the Union" (pp. 53–54) to answer questions 10–13.

10 The reader can tell from this article that Lincoln was —

F proud

G unfriendly

H determined

J cautious

11 Lincoln opposed Stephen A. Douglas because —

A Douglas attacked the newly formed Republican party

B Lincoln did not want slavery to become legal in the western territories

C Lincoln was an enemy to all Democrats

D Douglas wanted slavery to be permitted in the North

12 Paragraph 4 is important to the article because it —

F describes the challenges Lincoln faced as President

G explains why the North defeated the South in the Civil War

H discusses Lincoln's faults and weaknesses as President

J analyzes why the South withdrew from the Union

13 In paragraph 5, what does the author mean by the statement, "There were serious setbacks on the battlefield"?

A The lives of the soldiers on both sides were harsh and unpleasant.

B The soldiers had to retreat when the fighting became intense.

C There was a shortage of food and supplies for Lincoln's soldiers.

D The Union Army lost some battles and many soldiers were killed.

GO

Use "Jefferson Davis and the Confederacy" (pp. 54–55) to answer questions 14–17.

14 Davis went to a military academy because—

F he was an undisciplined youth

G many wealthy Southern families sent sons to such schools

H he wanted to serve in the army

J his parents thought he would receive a well-rounded education

15 Which of the following is the best summary of the article?

A Jefferson Davis began his career in the army. He fought with a Mississippi regiment and demonstrated bravery. Later, he got involved in politics and became the President of the Confederacy during the Civil War.

B Jefferson Davis was a popular Southern speaker and politician. He could have been President of the United States but instead chose to lead the Confederacy. Even after his top general conceded defeat, Davis wanted the South to keep fighting.

C Jefferson Davis was a Southern gentleman and army officer. He became a statesman in the mid-19th century, when the issues of states' rights and slavery dominated American politics. Davis led the Confederacy against the federal government. He served a short prison term and was well loved by the Southern people.

D Jefferson Davis attended military school. He was picked to be an officer during the Mexican War. He was brave and popular with his fellow Southerners, but was less successful as the President of the Confederacy.

16 From what the reader learns about Davis, which statement would not be reasonable?

F Davis believed that the federal government should have more power than the state governments.

G Davis was willing to take risks for the cause in which he believed.

H Davis was a persusavive speaker and a popular politician.

J Davis was disappointed when the Confederate Army surrendered.

17 Look at this flow chart showing the order of important events described in the article.

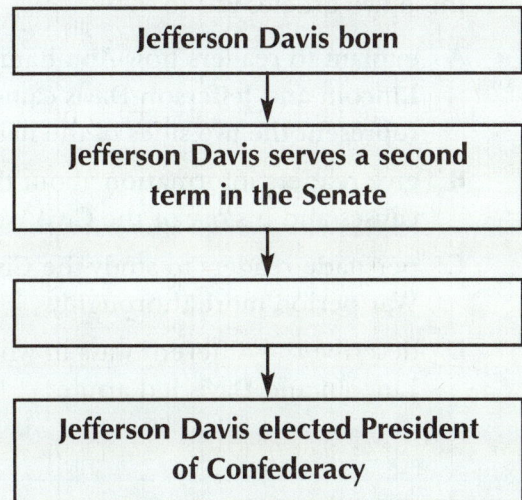

| Jefferson Davis born |
| Jefferson Davis serves a second term in the Senate |
| |
| Jefferson Davis elected President of Confederacy |

Which event belongs in the empty box?

A Jefferson Davis serves in the Mexican War

B The Civil War erupts

C Jefferson Davis refuses to run for President of the United States

D The Confederate Army surrenders

GO→

Use "Abraham Lincoln and the Union" and "Jefferson Davis and the Confederacy" to answer questions 18–21.

18 In each article, the author organizes information mainly by —

F comparing and contrasting two famous men who shaped America

G explaining the major differences between the North and the South

H showing how people today look back at the Civil War

J presenting important events in the lives of Lincoln and Davis in the order in which they took place

19 The most likely reason the author wrote these two articles was to —

A explain to readers how Abraham Lincoln and Jefferson Davis came to represent the two sides of the nation

B give readers information about the causes and history of the Civil War

C persuade readers to study the Civil War period more thoroughly

D describe the different ways in which Lincoln and Davis led armies

20 The advantage of reading these stories together is that it helps the reader understand how —

F slavery began in the United States

G the Union Army was able to defeat the Confederate Army

H customs in the North and South were different

J Abraham Lincoln and Jefferson Davis were natural leaders

21 Look at the diagram below, which shows information from both selections.

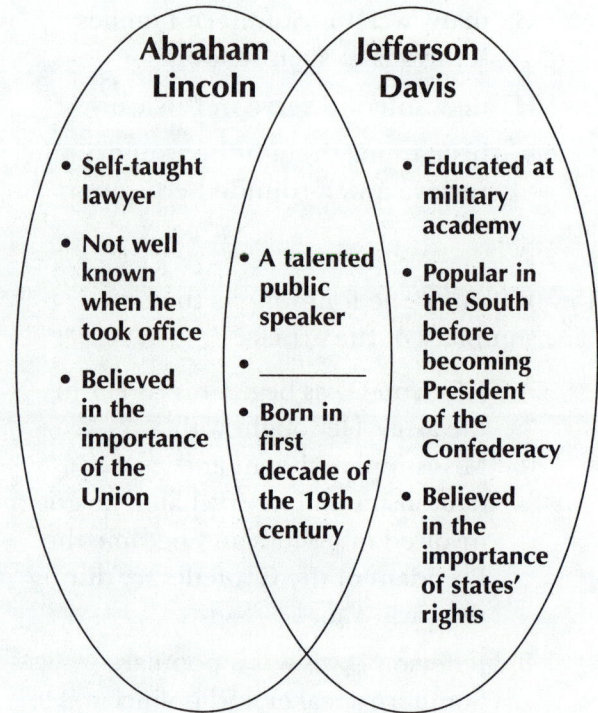

Abraham Lincoln
- Self-taught lawyer
- Not well known when he took office
- Believed in the importance of the Union

(overlap)
- A talented public speaker
- _____
- Born in first decade of the 19th century

Jefferson Davis
- Educated at military academy
- Popular in the South before becoming President of the Confederacy
- Believed in the importance of states' rights

Which statement belongs in the blank?

A Never wanted to serve as President

B Strong beliefs about slavery

C Had a successful career after the Civil War

D Trained as a professional soldier

GO ➤

DIRECTIONS: Carefully read the selection. Then answer the questions.

Louis Braille: Hope for the Blind

My notes about what I am reading

1   Louis Braille, the inventor of a reading and writing system for the blind, was born in Coupvray, France, in 1809. His father was a saddle maker. One day when Louis was three years old, he injured his eye while playing with a sharp tool from his father's workbench. Unfortunately, Louis was not treated by a doctor. Instead, an elderly woman from the village tried to treat his eye with home remedies, but the eye soon became infected. When the infection spread to Louis's other eye, he became blind.

2   This could have been a tragedy, but Louis Braille was intelligent and creative. He was lucky to be befriended by a priest, Jacques Palluy, and a schoolteacher, Antoine Becheret. These two men arranged for Louis to go to school in the village. Later, Louis was admitted to the Royal Institute for Blind Youth in Paris. He was the youngest child in the school and was often teased by his classmates. But he did very well at school, learning his academic subjects with the help of leather books printed with large, raised letters. He also learned practical crafts such as basketry and rope-making. The school made money from these goods and pupils graduated with enough practical skills to earn a living. In these years, Louis also studied music. He showed talent at the piano and organ, and sometimes performed for visitors at the school.

3   In 1821, a new director took over the running of the school and conditions were soon improved. Students were now taken out for fresh air at least twice a week. This was an important change because the cramped desks and stale air of the school building often made children ill. Tuberculosis, a lung disease, was widespread among the students.

4   The next important figure in Louis Braille's life was Charles Barbier de la Serre. This clever nobleman had escaped death at the hands of the mob during the French Revolution. He invented a secret code of writing that could be read by touch in the dark. The code was based on dots and dashes. Barbier

GO ➡

called his system of communication "sonography." He was convinced that the system would help the blind. The school's new director allowed students to experiment with the dots and dashes. The moment Louis touched the raised figures, he knew something wonderful had happened. He himself had tried to invent a kind of writing for the blind. Now he saw that it could be done.

5   Louis believed he could make a better <u>version</u> of Barbier's system. In 1824, at age fifteen, he solved the problem of reducing Barbier's twelve-dot cell to one using only six dots and a few dashes. The other students at the Royal Institute for Blind Youth loved the new system. But the teachers did not welcome the task of learning it for themselves. They all had normal sight and felt no urgency to learn another system.

6   Louis continued to develop his skills. He became the first blind apprentice teacher at the school when he was only seventeen. He also found work as a church organist. By 1828, he had combined his interests to come up with a way to copy music in his new system of writing. His book, *Method of Writing Words, Music, and Plain Songs by means of Dots, for Use by the Blind and Arranged for Them*, was published in 1829. Louis Braille was just twenty years old.

7   Louis became one of the first blind professors at the school. Eventually, other professors began to use Louis's alphabet to teach their students. Louis was a wonderful teacher who helped his pupils in many ways. He knew the importance of warm clothing and better living conditions; he had caught tuberculosis in the cold, dank school building. Despite poor health, Louis continued to teach and work on improving his code of writing. He also invented raphigraphy, an alphabet made of large print letters in dots, so that students could write letters to family members.

8   Louis Braille showed his work at the Paris Exhibition of Industry in 1834. The King of France himself, Louis Phillippe, discussed the invention with him. But few people understood what an important advance had been made. Over the years, Louis Braille would revise his textbook and continue to teach. When the school building was finally renovated, he recuperated

GO➤

from his long illness at home. On his return to teaching, a new director took over the Royal Institute for Blind Youth and prevented students from using the Braille method.

9   Students still used Braille in secret, though they were sometimes punished if caught with a Braille slate. When the new school building was dedicated, the director was finally convinced it was in his interest to allow a demonstration of Braille. Word of the new system began to spread throughout France. People began to realize that the blind would be more independent with a way to communicate. However, Louis Braille would not live to see his work become popular. He died in 1852, two years before France made Braille the official reading and writing system for the blind.

Use "Louis Braille: Hope for the Blind" (pp. 59–61) to answer questions 22–31.

---

22 Louis Braille's blindness was probably the result of —

    F other health problems that were discovered too late

    G the original injury to his eye

    H lack of proper medical treatment

    J unhealthy conditions in his father's workshop

23 Why was Louis allowed to attend the village school?

    A The schoolteacher and priest felt he could keep up with the students.

    B There were no other French schools willing to accept a blind student.

    C At first, people did not know that Louis was completely blind.

    D His father had requested that he study with regular students.

GO

24 Which sentence from the article best shows Louis's determination and ambition?

F *He was lucky to be befriended by a priest, Jacques Palluy, and a school teacher, Antoine Becheret.*

G *The next important figure in Louis Braille's life was Charles Barbier de la Serre.*

H *Despite poor health, Louis continued to teach and work on improving his code of writing.*

J *Louis Braille showed his work at the Paris Exhibition of Industry in 1834.*

25 In paragraph 5, the word <u>version</u> means —

A a new discovery

B a precise explanation of an idea

C a type of alphabet

D a form of something

26 The most likely reason the author wrote this article was to —

F explain the advances that have been made in teaching people with visual handicaps

G describe the miserable conditions in which blind people lived during the nineteenth century

H tell readers about Louis Braille and his contribution to the lives of blind people

J give readers information about Louis Braille and the alphabet used in his system

27 What can the reader tell about the Royal Institute for Blind Youth from reading this article?

A The students at the school were not particularly motivated.

B The building was uncomfortable and unhealthy for the students.

C Most of the school's teachers were blind or otherwise handicapped.

D The new director of the school was eager to experiment with new ideas.

28 The author organizes paragraph 8 of the article by —

F contrasting how people regarded Braille's work

G explaining the Braille method step-by-step

H presenting other methods of reading and writing used by blind people in the order of their invention

J describing step-by-step how Louis Braille improved his original system in later years

GO➡

29   Look at this web of information from the article.

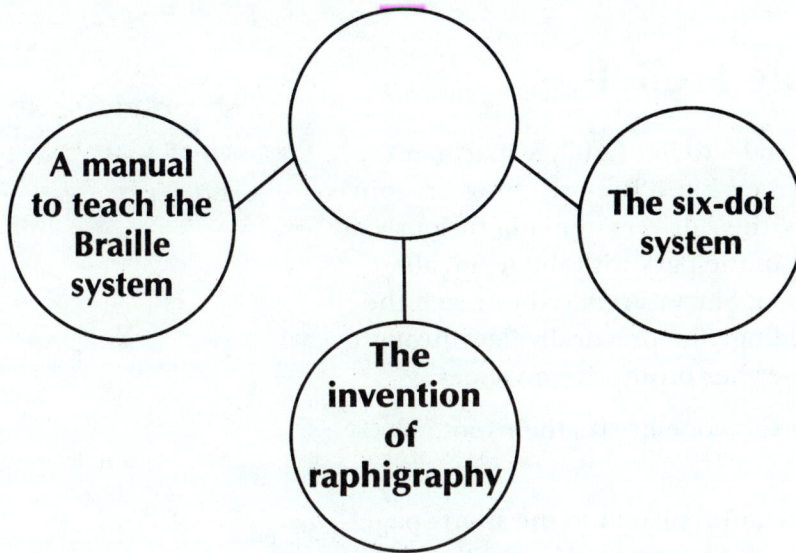

Which main idea belongs in the empty oval?

A   Famous inventions of the nineteenth century

B   Teaching methods at the Royal Institute for Blind Youth

C   Louis Braille's contributions to the blind

D   The Paris Exhibition of Industry

---

30   Most teachers at the school did not want to teach with the Braille method because —

F   they would first have to study Braille themselves

G   they did not believe the system worked

H   they thought that students would be unable to master it

J   they disliked Louis Braille and tried to ignore his work

31   This article is mainly about —

A   life at the Royal Institute for Blind Youth in Paris

B   the unhappy childhood of inventor Louis Braille

C   the challenges that many handicapped people must face

D   Louis Braille's efforts to improve communication for the blind

GO➤

DIRECTIONS: Carefully read the selection. Then answer the questions.

The Role Model

LaToya Phillips jogged up the stairs to her family's apartment. September heat hung over the streets like a fire-breathing dragon. The avenue was packed with cars, their drivers honking furiously at each other. After a four-mile run in the park with the team, all LaToya could think of was a shower. She was relieved to reach the cool lobby of her apartment building. She practically flew through the front door, nearly tripping over her brother's gym shoes.

"Kai, pick up your stuff before someone breaks their foot," she scolded.

Her younger brother shrugged and returned to the sports page of the newspaper. LaToya wondered if he ever read any other kind of printed material. Like herself, Kai loved sports: basketball, track, soccer—whatever the game, he was in it. But unlike LaToya, Kai needed to spend more time studying. His teachers always said he would be an "A" student with a little effort.

"What's in the paper?" she asked. "Don't get ice cream all over that. I want to look at it, too."

"Well, here's something. Some guy wrote a letter to the editor saying professional athletes were letting us kids down. He says it's all about money and status. Oh, and he claims that none of the guys who get basketball scholarships finish college. They either go to the pros or they wind up working in gas stations."

LaToya perched on the edge of the sofa. "Well, if that's true, it's a shame. Why would anyone waste their chance to get a college degree, and for free?"

"I guess they're too busy playing the game to hit the books," Kai answered.

At dinner, Mom asked the same old question: How was school today? Mom was a teacher, though not at the school LaToya and Kai attended. That was lucky because Mom was strict about their behavior. They would have had no chance to linger in the hallways between classes or order two pieces of pie for lunch with Mrs. Phillips hovering over them.

GO

My notes about what I am reading

"Okay," said Kai. "I passed my math test."

Mom patted his hand and gave him a piece of bread. LaToya pushed away her plate and sat there frowning until her mother had to ask her what was wrong. "It's this editorial in the paper. I just don't agree with it."

"Tell me about it," Mom suggested. So LaToya explained, with Kai interrupting every other second to add more details. Mom sat back and listened attentively and said she understood why they were both upset. They were both sports fans and could not stand to see any athlete harshly criticized.

LaToya objected. "If someone has done something wrong, I criticize them, too. But this writer talks as if kids haven't learned a lot from sports figures."

Mom poured herself some iced tea. "If you feel so strongly about the subject, why don't you compose your own editorial? I believe the paper might welcome a new voice. After all, editorials are a kind of dialogue."

LaToya stared doubtfully at her mother. "I just know that we've all learned from our athletes. But how can I prove it?"

"How about writing about one of your favorite sports figures? Sometimes an example is worth a thousand arguments."

Walking home from school the next afternoon, LaToya pondered this discussion. She enjoyed writing, yet she had the uneasy feeling that no newspaper editor would print a child's views. Suddenly, she stopped short, nearly tripping over a tree root that twisted itself over the pavement. What if she didn't <u>identify</u> herself as a sixth-grader? If her writing sounded mature enough, the editor might assume she was an adult. LaToya ran the home, eager to get to the computer. She was so absorbed in her work, she didn't even hear Kai bouncing his basketball against the wall or her mother clattering the pots and pans in the kitchen.

"Why don't you read me what you've written?" Mom invited her.

GO

My notes about what I am reading ✏️

Sports and Youth: Aren't We Forgetting Our Heroes?

I was shocked to read last week's editorial in this newspaper, "Hang Up Your Sneakers." The author stated that sports have become a business, and not a very nice one. He referred to some recent statistics on college basketball players, who supposedly fail to graduate within five years of admission to school. Further, the writer claims that athletes are poor influences on today's young people. He mentions drug use and dishonesty, as if these problems existed only in the world of sports. I believe that the writer has forgotten what athletes have given us.

Maybe one shining example will help us to remember. In 1998, Florence Griffith-Joyner passed away suddenly when she was only thirty-nine years old. Flo Jo began running track when she was seven and won the Jesse Owens National Youth Games at the age of fourteen. She attended the University of California, Los Angeles, where she continued running track. In 1984, she won a silver medal in the 200-meter dash during the 1984 Olympics. After a period of retirement, Flo Jo came back to win medals at the World Championship Games in Rome and the 1988 Olympic Games in Seoul, Korea. She set the world record in the 200-meter dash in the Olympic final, clocking in at 21.34.

Flo Jo combined speed, grace, beauty, and sportsmanship. When she ran in those gorgeous outfits that she designed herself, the crowds loved it. When she served as co-chairperson on the Council on Physical Fitness and Sports, we could respect her contribution. When she dedicated much of her time to coaching her husband, a champion jumper, we saw that she was a devoted wife and a good sport.

I ask you to think of other professional athletes who have combined sportsmanship with duty to others. It will not be hard to come up with a long list of names. Before we turn our backs on America's athletes, let's take a look at what they have given us.

"You've won me over," Mom smiled. "Did you ever think of joining the debating team as well as the track team?"

"No, but I'll think about it now," said LaToya proudly.

GO➡

Use "The Role Model" (pp. 64–66) to answer questions 32–40.

32 Read the dictionary entry below for the word <u>identify</u>.

identify \ ī den´ ə fī´ \ *v* **1.** to establish that someone or something is a particular person or thing **2.** to regard or treat as identical, or one and the same **3.** to be a means of knowing who or what a thing is **4.** to associate closely with something or someone

The meaning of the word <u>identify</u> in the story is most like which of the following definitions?

F Definition 1

G Definition 2

H Definition 3

J Definition 4

33 Which sentence from the story best shows that LaToya admires professional athletes?

A *"Why would anyone waste their chance to get a college degree, and for free?"*

B *LaToya pushed away her plate and sat there frowning until her mother had to ask her what was wrong.*

C *"I just know that we've all learned from our athletes."*

D *If her writing sounded mature enough, the editor might assume she was an adult.*

GO

34 The most likely setting for this story is —

F a large city

G a small town

H a suburb

J a rural area

35 LaToya and Kai are upset by the editorial in the newspaper because —

A they did not know that athletes do not always graduate from college

B they believe it does not present a fair view of athletes

C it does not mention their favorite sports figures

D the writer does not support his opinion with facts

36 The word <u>hovering</u> in the story is used to communicate a feeling of —

F comfort

G peacefulness

H watchfulness

J anger

37 The tone of LaToya's letter to the editor can best be described as —

A critical

B eager

C tense

D respectful

GO

38 LaToya was reluctant to write the editorial at first because —

F she did not think she was a good writer

G she did not believe the newspaper would publish it

H she was afraid she could not convince others of her viewpoint

J she was afraid that the writer of the published editorial was correct

39 Which statement from LaToya's editorial represents an opinion?

A *Flo Jo began running track when she was seven and won the Jesse Owens National Youth Games at the age of fourteen.*

B *She attended the University of California, Los Angeles, where she continued running track.*

C *She set the world record in the 200-meter dash in the Olympic final, clocking in at 21.34.*

D *Flo Jo combined speed, grace, beauty, and sportsmanship.*

40 Toward the end of the editorial, LaToya uses a series of statements beginning with "When" to —

F give the reader an exact timeline of Flo Jo's accomplishments

G provide details about the career of an athlete she admires

H use language in a strong and persuasive way

J compare Flo Jo to other champions in track

STOP

Writing DIRECTIONS: Read the introduction below. Then read the passage. Answer the questions that follow. Fill in the correct answers on your answer sheet.

PART 1: Revising and Editing

SAMPLE

Carmen wrote a letter to the editor expressing her opinion about something she read in the newspaper. She has asked you to help her revise and edit it. After you read Carmen's report, think about the suggestions you would make to help her correct and improve it. Then answer the questions that follow.

To the Editor:

(1) I was shocked to learn that so many languages were dying out. (2) A language is part of a people's culture and heritage. (3) Many words express concepts that are unique and special to a particular group. (4) When these words are forgotten, sometimes the concepts are too. (5) Surely there is something we can do to preserve these dying languages. (6) This is a greater loss that can never be recovered.

S-1 What is the BEST way to revise sentence 1?

A I am shocked to learn that so many languages were dying out.

B I was shocked to have learned that so many languages have been dying out.

C I was shocked to learn that so many languages are dying out.

D No revision is needed.

S-2 Which change, if any, should be made in sentence 6?

F Change *greater* to **great**

G Add a comma after *loss*

H Change *recovered* to **recover**

J Make no change

STOP

DIRECTIONS: Read the introduction below. Then read the passage. Answer the questions that follow. Fill in the correct answers on your answer sheet.

Rita is in the sixth grade. She wrote a report about the career that interests her. She has asked you to help her revise and edit it. After you read Rita's report, think about the suggestions you would make to help her correct and improve it. Then answer the questions that follow.

A Career in Broadcast Journalism

(1) One night last summer, me and my dad were watching the evening news together. (2) A news correspondent was giving her report on the situation in Serbia. (3) She spoke knowledgeably and intelligently about the war crimes trial at the Hague. (4) When I asked my father who the news reporter was, he told me she was Christiane Amanpour. (5) I quickly became a fan and followed her special reports on terrorism this year.

(6) I had never paid much attention to television news in the past. (7) I find myself watching the reports every evening with my parents. (8) Not only did I learn a lot about what goes on in the world, but I also discovered a new interest: the field of broadcast journalism. (9) I think people today want news right away. (10) It is true that you can find more details about a story by reading the newspaper. (11) On the other hand, television brings them news almost as quickly as it happens.

(12) I hope that someday I will have a career like Christiane Amanpour. (13) I'd love to travel to the scene of events and report the news to people back home. (14) Of course, first I realize that I will be needing special training and education. (15) A background in journalism are important. (16) Then I'd have to work hard to get a beginning job at a television station, that would be my first step. (17) Years from now, you might see me in some far-off part of the world with a microphone in my hand.

1 What change should be made in sentence 1?

   A Delete the comma after *summer*

   B Change *me and my dad* to **my dad and I**

   C Change *were* to **was**

   D Change *evening news* to **Evening News**

2 What change, if any, should be made in sentence 5?

   F Change *became* to **become**

   G Add a comma after *fan*

   H Change *special reports* to **Special Reports**

   J Make no change

3 Which transition word or phrase should be added to the beginning of sentence 7?

   A For instance,

   B And,

   C Before all this happens

   D But now

4 What change should be made to sentence 11?

   F Delete the comma after *hand*

   G Change *brings* to **will bring**

   H Change *them* to **us**

   J Change *happens* to **has happened**

5 Which sentence could be added after sentence 11 to support the ideas in the second paragraph (sentences 6–11)?

   A Radio is also of interest to me but not as much as television.

   B This is especially important when there is an emergency or a very important piece of news.

   C A reporter may have to travel for much of the year to cover stories.

   D Even a person who cannot read can follow a news story on television.

GO

6 Which of the following is the BEST way to rewrite the ideas in sentence 14?

F I realize of course that first I needed special training and education.

G Special training and education, of course, are needed, I realize, first.

H First, special training and education, of course, are needed as I realize.

J Of course, I realize that I would first need special training and education.

7 What change, if any, should be made in sentence 15?

A Add a comma after *background*

B Change *journalism* to **Journalism**

C Change *are* to **is**

D Make no change

8 What change should be made in sentence 16?

F Change *Then* to **Than**

G Change *I'd* to **I've**

H Add a comma after *hard*

J Change *that* to **which**

GO

DIRECTIONS: Read the introduction below. Then read the passage. Answer the questions that follow. Fill in the correct answers on your answer sheet.

Jorge is a sixth-grade student. He wants classmates to participate in the coming Earth Day festival and has prepared a paper about what Earth Day means. Jorge has asked you to help him revise and edit his paper. After you read Jorge's paper, think about the suggestions you would make to help him correct and improve it. Then answer the questions that follow.

Earth Day: It's for Everyone

(1) In 1970, a United States Senator from Wisconsin had a wonderful idea. (2) Senator Gaylord Nelson thought that Americans should get together to protest the abuse of the environment. (3) On April 22nd that year, millions of people found a common voice. (4) Groups concerned about environmental problems campaigned about these issues. (5) Earth Day helped people to realize that the earth is everyone's responsibility.

(6) Every spring, flowers budding and young animals being born. (7) It is a time of rebirth and new beginnings. (8) As we look around us, we should think about ways to portect this world. (9) They remind us that Earth is the only planet with living beings. (10) They point out that there are serious problems to be solved. (11) I propose that the students of Westburn Elementary School celebrates Earth Day on April 22nd, and every other day of the year as well.

(12) There are changes we can make right here in our school, our neighborhoods, and our town. (13) We can help recycle glass and metal used in

GO➤

school and at home. (14) We can use water wiser by running washing machines only when fully loaded and taking shorter showers. (15) We can urge our parents to attend town hall meetings about the environment. (16) We can also write to congressmen and senators about specific issues. (17) Earth Day is a great celebration that many people enjoy. (18) There are many holidays that bring people together. (19) But it should not be the only day of the year when we remember to care for the place where we live.

GO➤

9 What is the BEST way to combine sentences 3 and 4?

    A Millions of people on April 22nd that year found a common voice, campaigned about environmental problems.

    B On April 22nd that year, millions of people campaigned about environmental problems that found a common voice.

    C On April 22nd that year, millions of people found a common voice and campaigned about environmental problems.

    D On April 22nd that year, millions of people found a common voice, so they campaigned about environmental problems.

10 What is the BEST way to revise sentence 6?

    F Every spring, flowers bud and young animals are born.

    G Every spring, flowers are budding. Young animals are born.

    H Flowers budding and young animals being born every spring.

    J No revision is needed.

11 What change, if any, should be made in sentence 8?

    A Delete the comma after *us*

    B Change *portect* to **protect**

    C Change *world* to **World**

    D Make no change

12 The meaning of sentences 9 and 10 can be improved by changing the first *They* to —

    F Environmentalists

    G People

    H Students

    J News reporters

13 What change should be made in sentence 11?

    A Change *students* to **students'**

    B Change *School* to **school**

    C Change *celebrates* to **celebrate**

    D Add a comma after *on*

GO ▶

14 Which transition word or phrase should be added to the beginning of sentence 13?

F However,

G Actually,

H On the other hand,

J For example,

15 What change, if any, should be made in sentence 14?

A Change *wiser* to **wisely**

B Add a comma after **loaded**

C Change *shorter* to **shortly**

D Make no change

16 Which sentence does NOT belong in this essay?

F Sentence 7

G Sentence 11

H Sentence 17

J Sentence 18

STOP

PART II: Written Composition

> **Write a composition about a time when you made an important decision and explain the consequences of this decision.**

• • •

First, do some prewriting on the following two pages. Organize your composition and decide how you want to write it. Then write your composition on the two lined pages.

• • •

The information below will remind you of what to think about when you are writing your composition.

DON'T FORGET TO:

- ☐ write about why your decision was important and what happened as a result of this decision

- ☐ write an essay that will hold your reader's interest

- ☐ make sure that each sentence you write adds to your reader's understanding of your ideas

- ☐ express your ideas in a clear, direct way

- ☐ include appropriate details to help your reader fully understand your topic and purpose for writing

- ☐ proofread your work for correct spelling, capitalization, punctuation, grammar, and sentences

GO ➤

SPACE FOR PREWRITING

GO➤

SPACE FOR PREWRITING

GO ➤

81

82

STOP

TO THE PARENT

This section of the book is designed to ensure peak performance on the Texas Assessment of Knowledge and Skills in Mathematics. By offering grade-specific instruction, test-taking tips, and authentic practice, this book will help students approach the TAKS in Mathematics strategically and confidently.

This section includes content from the Texas Essential Knowledge and Skills (TEKS). The first part of the mathematics section contains modeled instruction with hints to guide students. The second part of the mathematics section contains a practice test that closely resembles the actual 6th-grade TAKS in Mathematics. In addition, the book provides a Mathematics Chart that matches the chart that will be given to students during the administration of the TAKS. This chart contains various formulas, measurement conversions, and rulers needed when taking the test. Your child may cut out this Mathematics Chart to use, or he or she may use a personal ruler. On the actual test, students are not permitted to use their own rulers.

There are two types of problems on the TAKS in Mathematics: multiple-choice items and griddable items.

Multiple-choice Items: The multiple-choice items are always followed by four answer choices. In the Modeled Instruction section, students mark their answers to multiple-choice items by filling in the circles at the bottom of the page. In the Test section, students mark their answers on a separate answer sheet.

Griddable Items: The griddable items are always followed by instructions that direct students to mark their answers in a grid like the one shown below. Students are required to write their answers in the space provided at the top of the grid and then fill in the correlating bubbles. In the Modeled Instruction section, grids will be provided directly below the griddable items for students to fill in. In the Test section, students mark their answers by filling in the grids on a separate answer sheet. More information about the griddable items is provided on the following pages of this answer key.

Griddable Items

There will be a few griddable items on the 6th-grade TAKS in Mathematics. These items will require that the student fill in a seven-column grid. This book provides seven-column grids for all griddable items. These grids closely correspond to those provided in the TAKS. Students may fill in solutions between 0 and 9,999.99. The fifth column from the left is a fixed decimal point. Students must mark digits in the correct columns in relation to this decimal position. A sheet of sample grids has been provided on the following page. It is recommended that you use this page to practice filling in grids with your child.

Here are some general rules to follow when answering griddable items:

- Print only one digit in each answer space at the top of the grid.
- Do not write digits or symbols outside the answer spaces.
- Mark digits in the correct columns in relation to the fixed decimal point.
- Write only numbers and never include the unit of measure (e.g., $, %, cm, in.).
- Write a zero in the answer space if the answer has a zero in it.
  Note: A blank answer space is not the same as a zero.
- Do not leave a blank answer space in the middle of an answer.
- Match numbers bubbled in each column to numbers written at the top of each column.
- Fill in answer bubbles completely and accurately with a solid black mark.
- Do not fill in any answer bubbles below blank answer spaces.

Here is an example of a griddable item with the grid correctly filled in:

Heather bought a jacket. She gave the cashier $120 and received change of $8.55. How much did the jacket cost?

Write your answer in the grid below. Fill in the bubbles. Remember to use the correct place value.

Note: It is not necessary to mark place-holding zeros before the answer (in this example, in the first column). However, if students do mark place-holding zeros, it will not affect the scoring of a response.

TAKS Griddable Item Practice Sheet

Introduction to the TAKS Mathematics Objectives

Included on the following pages are the six objectives designed specifically for the 6th-grade TAKS in Mathematics. Within each objective is a more specific breakdown of the knowledge and skills statements (which organize the objective) and the student expectations (or relevant TEKS that fit under that objective).

When preparing your child for the TAKS in Mathematics, it is important to accurately interpret the TAKS objectives and the information they encompass. This can be somewhat difficult, due to the complicated organization of a large amount of information. An excerpt of Objective 2 has been provided below to illustrate the breakdown of each objective into three parts.

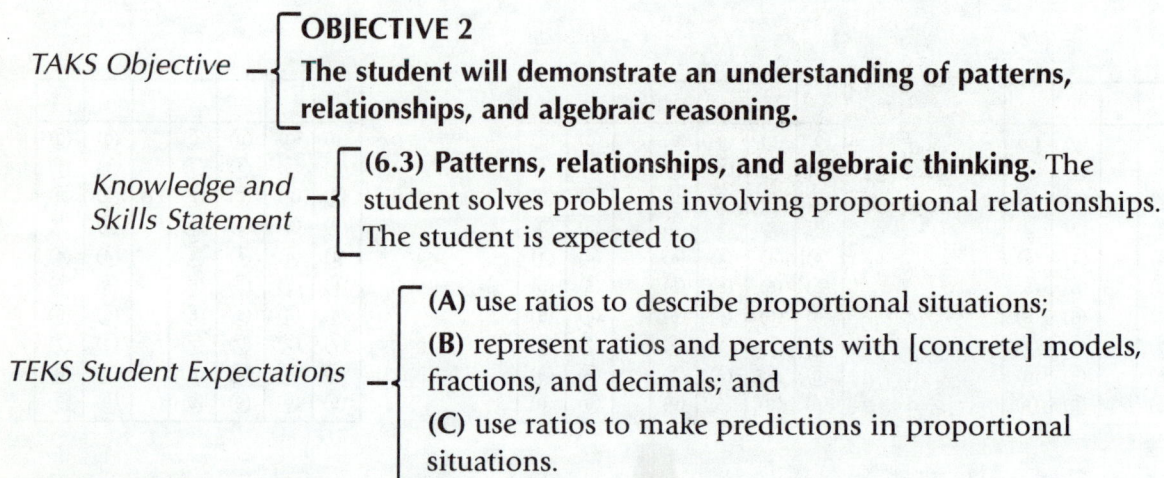

TAKS Objective —
OBJECTIVE 2
The student will demonstrate an understanding of patterns, relationships, and algebraic reasoning.

Knowledge and Skills Statement —
(6.3) Patterns, relationships, and algebraic thinking. The student solves problems involving proportional relationships. The student is expected to

TEKS Student Expectations —
(A) use ratios to describe proportional situations;

(B) represent ratios and percents with [concrete] models, fractions, and decimals; and

(C) use ratios to make predictions in proportional situations.

The number found before each knowledge and skills statement is the same identifying number of the statement in the TEKS. The "6" at the beginning of each number indicates that the knowledge and skills being tested are on the 6th-grade Mathematics level. Each statement broadly indicates the knowledge each student must attain and the skills they must master in order to successfully meet the TAKS evaluative criteria.

The TEKS student expectations outline exactly what a student must accomplish in order to demonstrate proficiency in the TAKS objectives and test. However, students will not be tested on all the information contained in each expectation. Any information contained in brackets will not be tested on the TAKS. See student expectation **(B)** in the sample above for an example of this exception. In addition, when the term *such as* is employed in a student expectation, it implies that the information following may or may not be tested, and that other information similar to that given may be assessed on the TAKS test. When the term *including* is used, it is far more likely that all information following will be assessed, though additional information similar to that given may also be tested on the TAKS.

On pages 87–89 you will find a detailed description of each of the six objectives that will be assessed on the 6th-grade TAKS in Mathematics. These descriptions will help you prepare your child for the TAKS. The descriptions will also help you assess your child's strengths and weaknesses as he or she works through the book.

On page 91 is a description of the objectives addressed to your child. You may wish to go over these objectives with your child.

OBJECTIVE 1

The student will demonstrate an understanding of numbers, operations, and quantitative reasoning.

(6.1) Number, operation, and quantitative reasoning. The student represents and uses rational numbers in a variety of equivalent forms. The student is expected to

(A) compare and order non-negative rational numbers;

(B) generate equivalent forms of rational numbers including whole numbers, fractions, and decimals;

(C) use integers to represent real-life situations;

(D) write prime factorizations using exponents; and

(E) identify factors and multiples including common factors and common multiples.

(6.2) Number, operation, and quantitative reasoning. The student adds, subtracts, multiplies, and divides to solve problems and justify solutions. The student is expected to

(A) model addition and subtraction situations involving fractions with [objects,] pictures, words, and numbers;

(B) use addition and subtraction to solve problems involving fractions and decimals;

(C) use multiplication and division of whole numbers to solve problems including situations involving equivalent ratios and rates; and

(D) estimate and round to approximate reasonable results and to solve problems where exact answers are not required.

OBJECTIVE 2

The student will demonstrate an understanding of patterns, relationships, and algebraic reasoning.

(6.3) Patterns, relationships, and algebraic thinking. The student solves problems involving proportional relationships. The student is expected to

(A) use ratios to describe proportional situations;

(B) represent ratios and percents with [concrete] models, fractions, and decimals; and

(C) use ratios to make predictions in proportional situations.

(6.4) Patterns, relationships, and algebraic thinking. The student uses letters as variables in mathematical expressions to describe how one quantity changes when a related quantity changes. The student is expected to

(A) use tables and symbols to represent and describe proportional and other relationships involving conversions, sequences, perimeter, area, etc.; and

(B) generate formulas to represent relationships involving perimeter, area, volume of a rectangular prism, etc., from a table of data.

(6.5) Patterns, relationships, and algebraic thinking. The student uses letters to represent an unknown in an equation. The student is expected to

(A) formulate an equation from a problem situation.

OBJECTIVE 3

The student will demonstrate an understanding of geometry and spatial reasoning.

(6.6) Geometry and spatial reasoning. The student uses geometric vocabulary to describe angles, polygons, and circles. The student is expected to

(A) use angle measurements to classify angles as acute, obtuse, or right;

(B) identify relationships involving angles in triangles and quadrilaterals; and

(C) describe the relationship between radius, diameter, and circumference of a circle.

(6.7) Geometry and spatial reasoning. The student uses coordinate geometry to identify location in two dimensions. The student is expected to

(A) locate and name points on a coordinate plane using ordered pairs of non-negative rational numbers.

OBJECTIVE 4

The student will demonstrate an understanding of the concepts and uses of measurement.

(6.8) Measurement. The student solves application problems involving estimation and measurement of length, area, time, temperature, capacity, weight, and angles. The student is expected to

(A) estimate measurements and evaluate reasonableness of results;

(B) select and use appropriate units, tools, or formulas to measure and to solve problems involving length (including perimeter and circumference), area, time, temperature, capacity, and weight;

(C) measure angles; and

(D) convert measures within the same measurement system (customary and metric) based on relationships between units.

OBJECTIVE 5

The student will demonstrate an understanding of probability and statistics.

(6.9) Probability and statistics. The student uses experimental and theoretical probability to make predictions. The student is expected to

(A) construct sample spaces using lists, tree diagrams, and combinations; and

(B) find the probabilities of a simple event and its complement and describe the relationship between the two.

(6.10) Probability and statistics. The student uses statistical representations to analyze data. The student is expected to

> **(A)** [draw and] compare different graphical representations of the same data;
>
> **(B)** use median, mode, and range to describe data;
>
> **(C)** sketch circle graphs to display data; and
>
> **(D)** solve problems by collecting, organizing, displaying, and interpreting data.

OBJECTIVE 6

The student will demonstrate an understanding of the mathematical processes and tools used in problem solving.

> **(6.11) Underlying processes and mathematical tools.** The student applies Grade 6 mathematics to solve problems connected to everyday experiences, investigations in other disciplines, and activities in and outside of school. The student is expected to
>
> > **(A)** identify and apply mathematics to everyday experiences, to activities in and outside of school, with other disciplines, and with other mathematical topics;
> >
> > **(B)** use a problem-solving model that incorporates understanding the problem, making a plan, carrying out the plan, and evaluating the solution for reasonableness; and
> >
> > **(C)** select or develop an appropriate problem-solving strategy from a variety of different types, including drawing a picture, looking for a pattern, systematic guessing and checking, acting it out, making a table, working a simpler problem, or working backwards to solve a problem.

(6.12) Underlying processes and mathematical tools. The student communicates about Grade 6 mathematics through informal and mathematical language, representations, and models. The student is expected to

> **(A)** communicate mathematical ideas using language, efficient tools, appropriate units, and graphical, numerical, physical, or algebraic mathematical models.

(6.13) Underlying processes and mathematical tools. The student uses logical reasoning to make conjectures and verify conclusions. The student is expected to

> **(A)** make conjectures from patterns or sets of examples and nonexamples; and
>
> **(B)** validate his/her conclusions using mathematical properties and relationships.

TO THE STUDENT

The 6th-grade TAKS in Mathematics is designed to test your math skills over 6 different objectives, listed on page 91 of this book. Review these objectives before moving on, in order to familiarize yourself with what the state will be testing you on.

The test will include two types of problems: multiple-choice items and griddable items.

Multiple-choice Items

You are already familiar with multiple-choice items. There are four answer choices after each problem. In the Modeled Instruction section, at the bottom of the page are circles with a letter in each. You need to fill in the circle of the solution. For the test, you are required to fill in your solution on a separate answer sheet. Remember to pick the choice that you think is the best answer. Some problems will have an answer choice that states "Not Here." This means that the correct solution is not given in any of the answer choices. Fill in the circle for "Not Here" if you do not find the solution in any of the answer choices.

Griddable Items

You may not be as familiar with the griddable items on this test. For these problems, you are given a blank, 7-column grid. You are required to fill in the grid with the correct solution to the problem. Fill in the grid as completely as possible. In the Modeled Instruction section, the grids are included with the problems. When you take the test, you will fill in the grids on a separate answer sheet. The grid may be filled in using a few correct ways, which are explained on pages 83–84. The answer must be printed in the answer boxes, and the matching bubbles under the answer boxes should be filled in. Here is an example of the grid that you will see on the 6th-grade TAKS in Mathematics:

OBJECTIVE 1:   The student will demonstrate an understanding of numbers, operations, and quantitative reasoning.

OBJECTIVE 2:   The student will demonstrate an understanding of patterns, relationships, and algebraic reasoning.

OBJECTIVE 3:   The student will demonstrate an understanding of geometry and spatial reasoning.

OBJECTIVE 4:   The student will demonstrate an understanding of the concepts and uses of measurement.

OBJECTIVE 5:   The student will demonstrate an understanding of probability and statistics.

OBJECTIVE 6:   The student will demonstrate an understanding of the mathematical processes and tools used in problem solving.

OBJECTIVE 1
The student will demonstrate an understanding of numbers, operations, and quantitative reasoning.

DIRECTIONS: Read each question and choose the best answer. For the multiple-choice items, fill in the circle at the bottom of the page for the answer you have chosen. If the correct answer is not available, mark the letter for "Not Here." For the griddable item, fill in the grid completely with the correct answer.

1 A laser printer can print 12 pages per minute. At this rate, how long will it take the printer to print 300 pages?

A 288 minutes

B 30 minutes

C 25 minutes

D 20 minutes

HINT
You can use division to solve this problem.

Objective 1 (6.2)(C): *The student is expected to use multiplication and division of whole numbers to solve problems including situations involving equivalent ratios and rates.*

2 Kaitlin placed 0.568, $\frac{3}{4}$, $1\frac{1}{3}$, and 0.81 on a number line. Which number is closest to 0?

F 0.568

G $\frac{3}{4}$

H $1\frac{1}{3}$

J 0.81

HINT
Convert the fraction and mixed number to decimals so that you can compare the four choices. Then work from left to right to compare the place values of the numbers.

Objective 1 (6.1)(A): *The student is expected to compare and order non-negative rational numbers.*

1 Ⓐ Ⓑ Ⓒ Ⓓ **2** Ⓕ Ⓖ Ⓗ Ⓙ

GO

3 Which number is NOT a common multiple of 3 and 9?

    A 18

    B 27

    C 36

    D 39

HINT
You multiply a number by 1, 2, 3, 4,… to find its multiples. A common multiple of two numbers is a multiple that both numbers have.

Objective 1 (6.1)(E): *The student is expected to identify factors and multiples including common factors and common multiples.*

4 Which is the prime factorization of 60?

    F $3 \times 4 \times 5$

    G $2^2 \times 3 \times 5$

    H $2 \times 3^2 \times 5$

    J Not Here

HINT
You can use a tree diagram to find the prime factorization of a number. Begin by finding any pair of factors. Then break down each of those numbers into a pair of factors. Continue the process until prime factors are reached.

Objective 1 (6.1)(D): *The student is expected to write prime factorizations using exponents.*

5 Jacob is painting his kitchen. He completed $\frac{1}{2}$ of the job on Monday and $\frac{1}{3}$ of the job on Tuesday. Which diagram can be used to model the part of the job Jacob did in all on Monday and Tuesday?

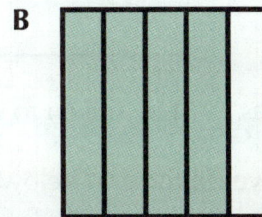

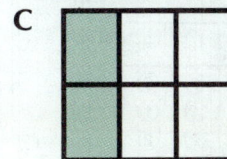

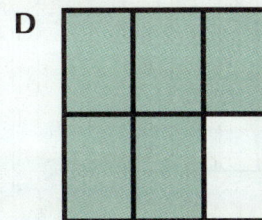

A

B

C

D

HINT
To model fractions with different denominators on the same diagram, first find a common denominator for the fractions.

Objective 1 (6.2)(A): *The student is expected to model addition and subtraction situations involving fractions with [objects,] pictures, words, and numbers.*

GO➤

3 Ⓐ Ⓑ Ⓒ Ⓓ | **4** Ⓕ Ⓖ Ⓗ Ⓙ | **5** Ⓐ Ⓑ Ⓒ Ⓓ

6 Use the portion of the road map below.

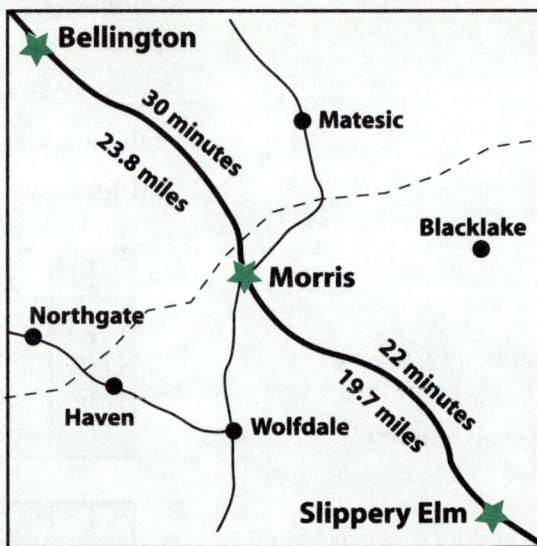

How many miles must be driven to go from Bellington to Slippery Elm?

Write your answer in the grid below. Fill in the bubbles. Remember to use the correct place value.

💡 **HINT**

Begin by making sure you understand how the map is labeled. Find the towns of Bellington and Slippery Elm, and how they are connected by roads. You must add decimals to find the total distance.

Objective 1 (6.2)(B): *The student is expected to use addition and subtraction to solve problems involving fractions and decimals.*

OBJECTIVE 2

The student will demonstrate an understanding of patterns, relationships, and algebraic reasoning.

DIRECTIONS: Read each question and choose the best answer. For the multiple-choice items, fill in the circle at the bottom of the page for the answer you have chosen. If the correct answer is not available, mark the letter for "Not Here." For the griddable item, fill in the grid completely with the correct answer.

1 Look at the number pattern in the box.

| 12, 24, 36, 48, ... |

Which number sentence can be used to find n, the ninth number in the pattern?

A $n = 48 \times 9$

B $n = 48 + 9$

C $n = 12 \times 9$

D $n = 12 + 9$

💡 **HINT**
You can examine the number pattern and try to find the rule yourself. Or you can examine the answer choices and test each one on the number pattern.

Objective 2 (6.4)(A): *The student is expected to use tables and symbols to represent and describe proportional and other relationships involving conversions, sequences, perimeter, area, etc.*

2 A survey of 50 students finds that 19 are in favor of changing the time school begins and ends each day. There are 650 students in this school. Based on the survey, what is the best prediction of the total number of students who are in favor of changing the time school begins and ends each day?

Write your answer in the grid below. Fill in the bubbles. Remember to use the correct place value.

💡 **HINT**
First write the ratio of students that are in favor of the change. Then set up and solve a proportion to find the predicted number of students.

Objective 2 (6.3)(C): *The student is expected to use ratios to make predictions in proportional situations.*

GO➤

3 The table below shows the measurement for three rectangles. Each has a width of 2 cm.

Perimeter of Rectangles		
width	length	perimeter
2 cm	3 cm	10 cm
2 cm	4 cm	12 cm
2 cm	5 cm	14 cm

Which formula could be used to find *P*, the perimeter of a rectangle, whose width is 2 cm and length is 12 cm?

F $P = 2 + 2 \times 12$

G $P = 4 + 2 \times 12$

H $P = 2 + 12$

J $P = 4 + 12$

HINT
Perimeter is the total distance around a figure.

Objective 2 (6.4)(B): *The student is expected to generate formulas to represent relationships involving perimeter, area, volume of a rectangular prism, etc., from a table of data.*

4 The triangles shown below are proportional.

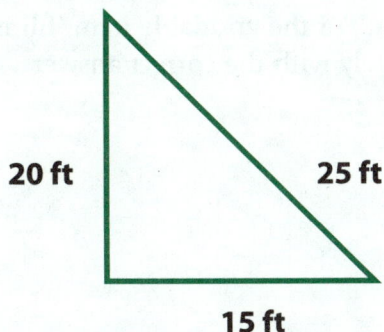

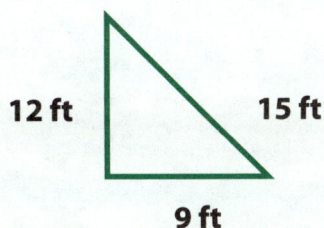

20 ft   25 ft

15 ft

12 ft   15 ft

9 ft

What is the ratio of a side length of the smaller triangle to the corresponding side length of the larger triangle?

A 5 to 3

B 3 to 5

C 3 to 4 to 5

D Not Here

💡 **HINT**

Focus on a side from one triangle and its corresponding side from the other triangle. Then write the ratio of their lengths in simplest form.

Objective 2 (6.3)(A): *The student is expected to use ratios to describe proportional situations.*

5 Janet bought 6 boxes of doughnuts for a breakfast meeting. There are 12 doughnuts in a box. The people at the meeting ate all but 4 of the doughnuts. Which equation can be used to find *d*, the number of doughnuts that were eaten?

F $d = 6 \times 12 - 4$

G $d = 6 \times 12 - 4 \times 12$

H $d = 2 \times 12$

J $d = 6 \times (12 - 4)$

💡 **HINT**

Read the problem more than once to make sure you understand exactly what it is describing. Once you understand the situation, think about how you would solve it. Then see if one of the equations matches your method.

Objective 2 (6.5)(A): *The student is expected to formulate an equation from a problem situation.*

4 Ⓐ Ⓑ Ⓒ Ⓓ | 5 Ⓕ Ⓖ Ⓗ Ⓙ

STOP

O BJECTIVE 3
The student will demonstrate an understanding of geometry and spatial reasoning.

DIRECTIONS: Read each question and choose the best answer. For the multiple-choice items, fill in the circle at the bottom of the page for the answer you have chosen. For the griddable item, fill in the grid completely with the correct answer.

1 The three sides of the triangle below are equal in length.

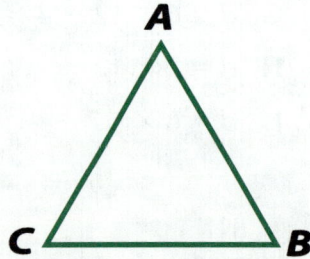

A
C   B

How many degrees are in angle A?

Write your answer in the grid below. Fill in the bubbles.
Remember to use the correct place value.

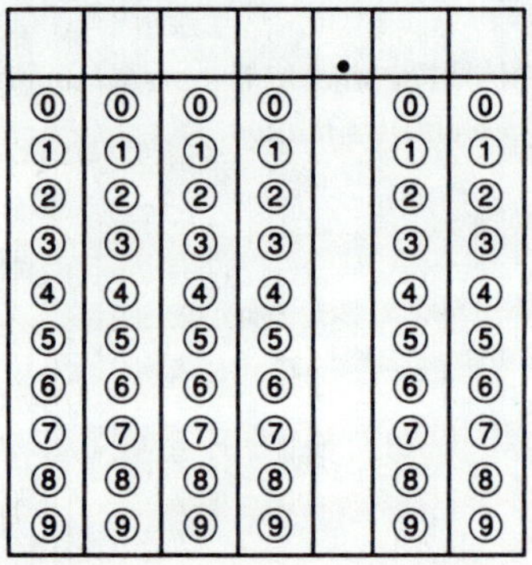

[grid with bubbles 0-9]

💡 **HINT**
The measures of the three angles of a triangle must add up to 180°.

Objective 3 (6.6)(B): *The student is expected to identify relationships involving angles in triangles and quadrilaterals.*

1 Griddable Item

GO

2 A circular swimming pool has a diameter of *d* feet.

d feet

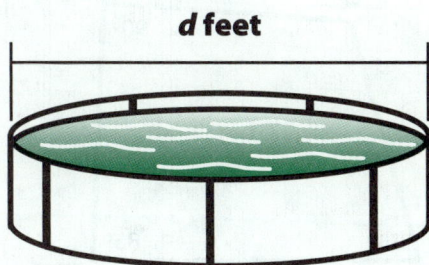

About how far is the distance around the outside of the pool?

A A little more than 6*d* feet

B A little less than 6*d* feet

C A little more than 3*d* feet

D A little less than 3*d* feet

💡 **HINT**
The circumference of a circle measures the distance around it. Circumference is related to diameter by the formula $C = \pi \times d$.

Objective 3 (6.6)(C): *The student is expected to describe the relationship between radius, diameter, and circumference of a circle.*

3 Which point best represents the ordered pair (3, 4) on the coordinate grid below?

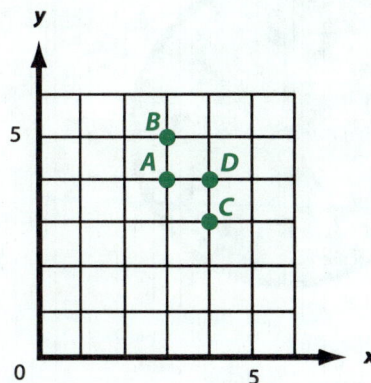

F Point *A*

G Point *B*

H Point *C*

J Point *D*

💡 **HINT**
To graph an ordered pair, start at (0, 0). The first number in the ordered pair tells you how far to move to the right. The second number in the ordered pair tells you how far to move up.

Objective 3 (6.7)(A): *The student is expected to locate and name points on a coordinate plane using ordered pairs of non-negative rational numbers.*

GO➤

2 Ⓐ Ⓑ Ⓒ Ⓓ | **3** Ⓕ Ⓖ Ⓗ Ⓙ

4 What type of angle is formed by the hands of the clock below at 7:00?

A Acute

B Obtuse

C Right

D Straight

💡 **HINT**
An acute angle is between 0° and 90°. A right angle is 90°. An obtuse angle is between 90° and 180°. A straight angle is 180°.

Objective 3 (6.6)(A): *The student is expected to use angle measurements to classify angles as acute, obtuse, or right.*

5 QRST is a quadrilateral.

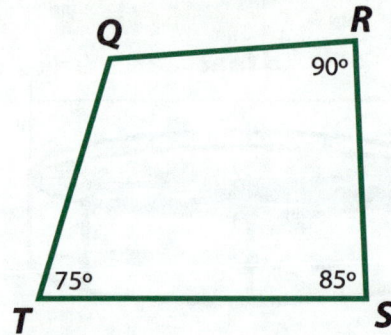

What is the measure of ∠Q?

F 85°

G 90°

H 105°

J 110°

💡 **HINT**
Use the fact that the sum of the measures of the angles of QRST must equal 360°.

Objective 3 (6.6)(B): *The student is expected to identify relationships involving angles in triangles and quadrilaterals.*

OBJECTIVE 4

The student will demonstrate an understanding of the concepts and uses of measurement.

DIRECTIONS: Read each question and choose the best answer. For the multiple-choice items, fill in the circle at the bottom of the page for the answer you have chosen. If the correct answer is not available, mark the letter for "Not Here." For the griddable item, fill in the grid completely with the correct answer.

1 What is the measure of ∠ABC, to the nearest degree?

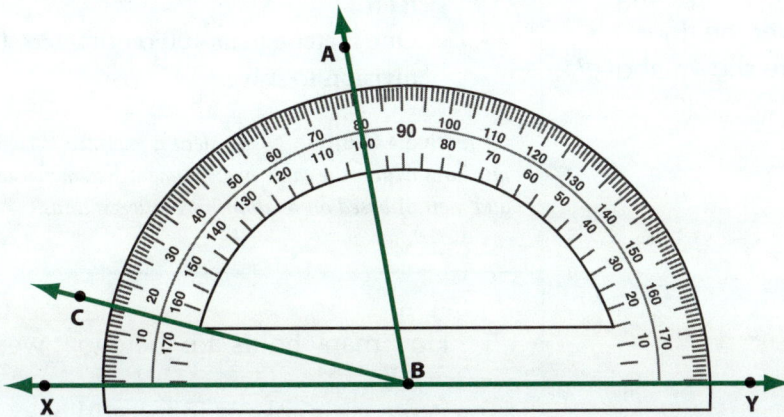

A 15°

B 65°

C 80°

D 95°

💡 **HINT**
Find the number where $\overrightarrow{BC}$ crosses the outside edge of the protractor. Subtract that from the number where $\overrightarrow{BA}$ crosses the outside edge of the protractor.

Objective 4 (6.8)(C): The student is expected to measure angles.

---

2 What is the approximate circumference of the circle shown below?

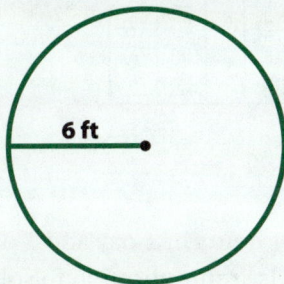

6 ft

F 18.84 ft   H 30.84 ft
G 20.84 ft   J 37.68 ft

💡 **HINT**
Circumference is related to radius according to the formula $C = 2 \times \pi \times r$.

Objective 4 (6.8)(B): The student is expected to select and use appropriate units, tools, or formulas to measure and to solve problems involving length (including perimeter and circumference), area, time, temperature, capacity, and weight.

GO ➡️

1 Ⓐ Ⓑ Ⓒ Ⓓ | 2 Ⓕ Ⓖ Ⓗ Ⓙ

3 Carpeting is sold by the square yard.

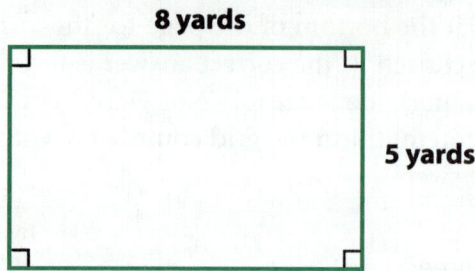

8 yards

5 yards

How many square yards of carpeting does Rhoda need to cover the floor whose measurements are shown above?

A 13 square yards

B 26 square yards

C 40 square yards

D 80 square yards

HINT
The area of a rectangle is found by using the formula Area = length × width.

Objective 4 (6.8)(B): *The student is expected to select and use appropriate units, tools, or formulas to measure and to solve problems involving length (including perimeter and circumference), area, time, temperature, capacity, and weight.*

4 A snail crawled 85 centimeters. How many meters did the snail crawl?

F 0.85 m

G 8.5 m

H 8,500 m

J Not Here

HINT:
One meter equals 100 centimeters. Use division to solve.

Objective 4 (6.8)(D): *The student is expected to convert measures within the same measurement system (customary and metric) based on relationships between units.*

5 How many hours are there in 2 weeks?

Write your answer in the grid below. Fill in the bubbles. Remember to use the correct place value.

				•		
⓪	⓪	⓪	⓪		⓪	⓪
①	①	①	①		①	①
②	②	②	②		②	②
③	③	③	③		③	③
④	④	④	④		④	④
⑤	⑤	⑤	⑤		⑤	⑤
⑥	⑥	⑥	⑥		⑥	⑥
⑦	⑦	⑦	⑦		⑦	⑦
⑧	⑧	⑧	⑧		⑧	⑧
⑨	⑨	⑨	⑨		⑨	⑨

HINT
There are 24 hours in 1 day and 7 days in 1 week. Use multiplication to solve.

Objective 4 (6.8)(D): *The student is expected to convert measures within the same measurement system (customary and metric) based on relationships between units.*

GO

6 Use the ruler on the Mathematics Chart to measure the perimeter of this triangle. Which is the best estimate of the perimeter of the triangle?

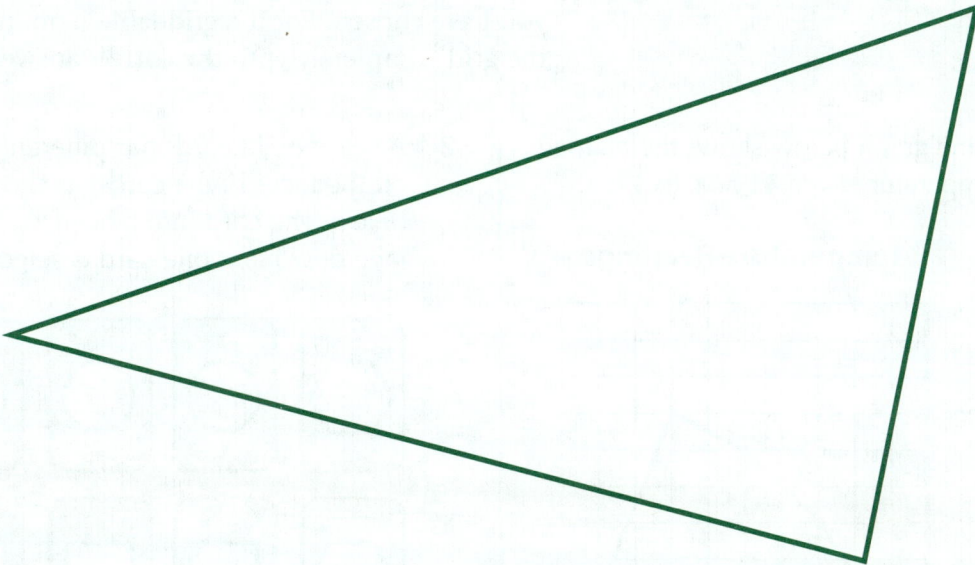

A 23 cm

B 28 cm

C 33 cm

D 38 cm

💡 **HINT**

Perimeter is the distance around the triangle. Use your centimeter ruler from the Mathematics Chart to measure each side's length and add the lengths together. Round your answer.

Objective 4 (6.8)(A): *The student is expected to estimate measurements and evaluate reasonableness of results.*

6 Ⓐ Ⓑ Ⓒ Ⓓ

STOP

OBJECTIVE 5
The student will demonstrate an understanding of probability and statistics.

DIRECTIONS: Read each question and choose the best answer. For the multiple-choice items, fill in the circle at the bottom of the page for the answer you have chosen. For the griddable item, fill in the grid completely with the correct answer.

1 The line graph below shows the change in temperature from 11 A.M. to 3 P.M.

Temperature Readings

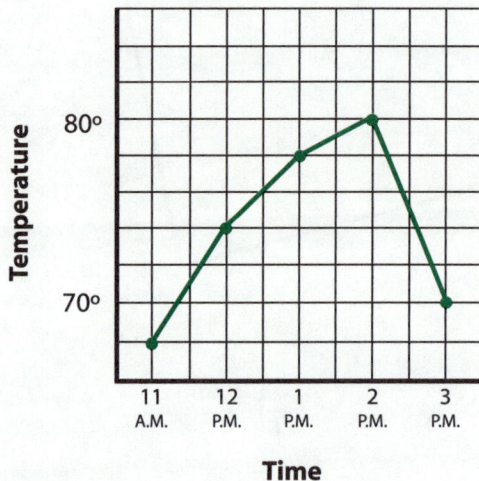

Time

Between which two hours did the temperature increase by the greatest amount?

A 11 A.M. and 12 P.M.

B 12 P.M. and 1 P.M.

C 1 P.M. and 2 P.M.

D 2 P.M. and 3 P.M.

HINT
Find the temperatures at each of the hours given on the graph. The greatest increase in temperature is where the line segment has the steepest rise.

Objective 5 (6.10)(D): *The student is expected to solve problems by collecting, organizing, displaying, and interpreting data.*

2 A set of eight cards has different shapes on the faces of the cards, as shown below. The cards are placed face down and one card is selected.

What is the probability that the card does NOT have a circle on its face?

F $\frac{3}{8}$

G $\frac{5}{8}$

H $\frac{1}{3}$

J $\frac{2}{3}$

HINT
P (event NOT occurring) $= 1 - P$ (event occurring). Begin by finding the probability that the card selected has a circle on its face.

Objective 5 (6.9)(B): *The student is expected to find the probabilities of a simple event and its complement and describe the relationship between the two.*

1 Ⓐ Ⓑ Ⓒ Ⓓ   2 Ⓕ Ⓖ Ⓗ Ⓙ

3 The pointer on the spinner shown below is spun twice.

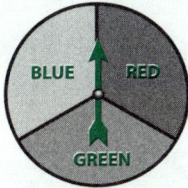

Which tree diagram shows all the possible outcomes for the two spins?

A

- Red
- Blue
- Green

B

- Red
  - Blue
  - Green
- Blue
  - Red
  - Green
- Green
  - Red
  - Blue

C

- Red
  - Red
  - Red
  - Red
- Blue
  - Blue
  - Blue
  - Blue
- Green
  - Green
  - Green
  - Green

D

- Red
  - Red
  - Blue
  - Green
- Blue
  - Red
  - Blue
  - Green
- Green
  - Red
  - Blue
  - Green

💡 **HINT**
There are three outcomes for the first spin and three outcomes for the second spin.

Objective 5 (6.9)(A): *The student is expected to construct sample spaces using lists, tree diagrams, and combinations.*

---

4 A high-school basketball team has twelve players. Their ages are shown in the table below.

Age	Number of Players
18	4
17	3
16	2
15	2
14	1

What is the median age of the players on this team?

Write your answer in the grid below. Fill in the bubbles. Remember to use the correct place value.

💡 **HINT**
The median is the middle number in a data set that has been ordered. If the data set has an even amount of numbers, the median is the average of the two middle numbers. Here, the data consists of the ages of the 12 players. The median is the average of the 6th and 7th age.

Objective 5 (6.10)(B): *The student is expected to use median, mode, and range to describe data.*

5 In the year 2001, the population of the United States reached 284 million. The table below shows a breakdown of state population.

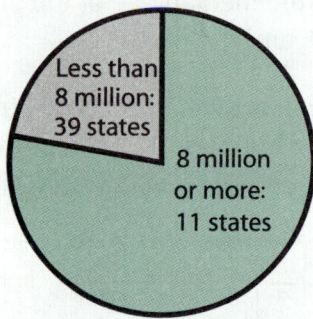

States with population 8 million or more	11
States with population less than 8 million	39

Which circle graph best displays the data shown in the table?

F **State Population**

Less than 8 million: 39 states

8 million or more: 11 states

H **State Population**

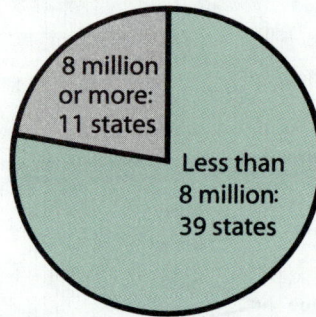

8 million or more: 11 states

Less than 8 million: 39 states

G **State Population**

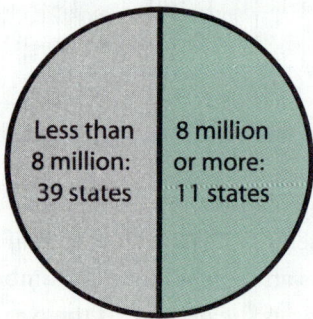

Less than 8 million: 39 states

8 million or more: 11 states

J **State Population**

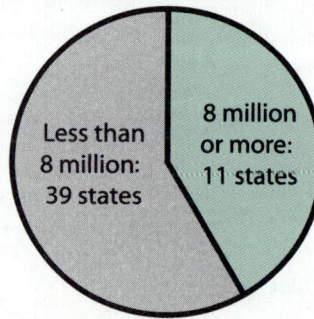

Less than 8 million: 39 states

8 million or more: 11 states

💡 **HINT**

Look at the data in the table and think in terms of percent: About what percent of the whole does each category represent? Then find the graph whose two sections best match those percents.

Objective 5 (6.10)(C): *The student is expected to sketch circle graphs to display data.*

5 Ⓕ Ⓖ Ⓗ Ⓙ

◉BJECTIVE 6

The student will demonstrate an understanding of the mathematical processes and tools used in problem solving.

DIRECTIONS: Read each question and choose the best answer. For the multiple-choice items, fill in the circle at the bottom of the page for the answer you have chosen. If the correct answer is not available, mark the letter for "Not Here." For the griddable item, fill in the grid completely with the correct answer.

1 Caroline divided the counting numbers into two groups according to a rule. Her rule is related to the prime factors a number has. The way in which the whole numbers from 2 to 20 fall into the two groups is shown below.

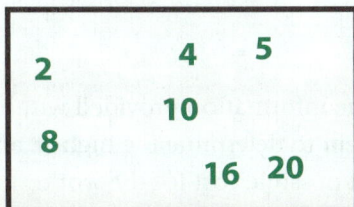

GROUP A

2   4   5
         10
8
      16   20

GROUP B

    3   7
       6
9   11   13   14
      12
15   17   18   19

What is the next number that Caroline will place in Group *A*?

Write your answer in the grid below. Fill in the bubbles.
Remember to use the correct place value.

💡 **HINT**

Look at the numbers in Group *A* and find their prime factors.
What do all the numbers have in common?

Objective 6 (6.13)(A): *The student is expected to make conjectures from patterns or sets of examples and nonexamples.*

GO ➡

1 Griddable Item

2 Ben used 4.5 gallons of gas driving his car from Loudon to Kippinger Falls. When he left Loudon, his odometer read 4,892.8 miles. When he arrived in Kippinger Falls 2 hours 45 minutes later, his odometer read 5,020.1 miles. Which of the following can NOT be determined from the information given?

A   The number of miles Ben drove

B   Ben's average speed during the trip

C   The number of miles per gallon Ben's car got on the trip

D   The time at which Ben left Loudon

💡 **HINT**
Read the problem carefully. Then eliminate the answer choices that you can determine.

Objective 6 (6.11)(B): *The student is expected to use a problem-solving model that incorporates understanding the problem, making a plan, carrying out the plan, and evaluating the solution for reasonableness.*

3 Emma is having her car's brakes repaired. The mechanic charges $65 per hour for labor and the job should take 90 minutes. The parts needed cost between $40 and $60. Which of these is an amount Emma might expect to pay for this work?

F $150

G $165

H $180

J $195

💡 **HINT**
Use the information provided within the problem to determine the highest and lowest possible cost for the work.

Objective 6 (6.11)(A): *The student is expected to identify and apply mathematics to everyday experiences, to activities in and outside of school, with other disciplines, and with other mathematical topics.*

4   Which equation does the drawing shown below represent?

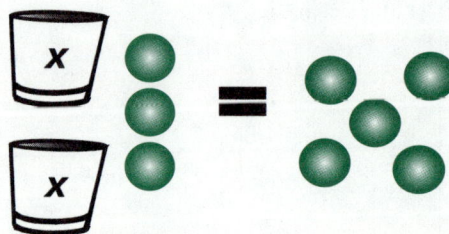

A $5x = 5$ C $2x + 3 = 5$

B $2x + 3 = 5x$ D   Not Here

💡 **HINT**
Each of the shaded circles stands for the number 1. The cups marked x can be added together to form $2x$.

Objective 6 (6.12)(A): *The student is expected to communicate mathematical ideas using language, efficient tools, appropriate units, and graphical, numerical, physical, or algebraic models.*

5 A regular octagon has eight sides of equal length and eight angles of equal measure. Derek wants to find the area of the regular octagon below. Derek does not know the formula for the area of a regular octagon. But he does know the formulas for the area of a rectangle, the area of a triangle, and the area of a trapezoid. He decides to break the octagon into smaller figures whose areas he can calculate.

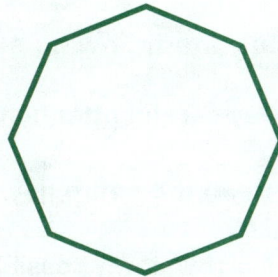

Which diagram is NOT appropriate for Derek to use?

F

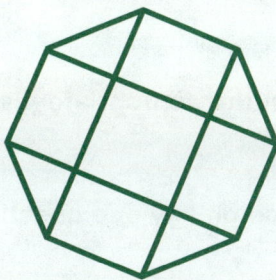

H

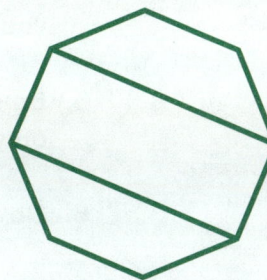

G

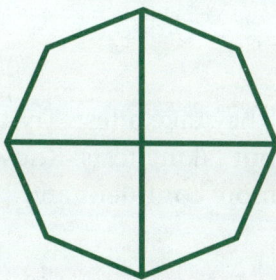

J

💡 **HINT**

Derek knows how to find the areas of rectangles, triangles, and trapezoids. So, he can find the area of any diagram that contains only those figures.

Objective 6 (6.11)(C): *The student is expected to select or describe an appropriate problem-solving strategy from a variety of different types, including drawing a picture, looking for a pattern, systematic guessing and checking, acting it out, making a table, working a simpler problem, or working backwards to solve a problem.*

5 Ⓕ Ⓖ Ⓗ Ⓙ

STOP

Now you will take a practice test. The skills and hints you have learned in the first section of this book will help you succeed on this test. Be sure to follow the directions. Read everything carefully and think about your answers before responding.

> **Try using the following strategies as you take the test:**
>
> 1. **Pay careful attention to directions.**
>
> 2. **Read the entire question and all the choices.**
>
> 3. **Narrow down possible answers by eliminating choices that are clearly incorrect.**
>
> 4. **Use the space around the questions to work out your answer.**
>
> 5. **Be sure to mark answers in the appropriate place on your answer sheet.**
>
> 6. **Do not spend too much time on any one question.**
>
> 7. **Mark items to return to if time permits.**
>
> 8. **Use any time remaining to review answers.**

Sometimes people get nervous when they take a test. Try to remember what you have learned about taking tests. Knowing what to expect should help you feel more confident and improve your score.

Remember to use the separate answer sheet on page 142 to fill in your answers.

DIRECTIONS: Read each question and choose the best answer. For the multiple-choice items, fill in the circle on your answer sheet for the answer you have chosen. If the correct answer is not available, mark the letter for "Not Here." For the griddable items, fill in the grid completely with the correct answer.

SAMPLE A

How is 15% written as a fraction?

A $\frac{15}{1}$

B $\frac{3}{2}$

C $\frac{3}{20}$

D $\frac{3}{200}$

SAMPLE B

Jan has the coins shown below, in his pocket.

If Jan selects a coin without looking, what is the probability in decimal form that the coin selected is NOT a nickel?

Write your answer in the grid on your answer sheet. Fill in the bubbles. Remember to use the correct place value.

STOP

1 On January 24, 1839, the Lone Star Flag was adopted as the national flag of the Republic of Texas.

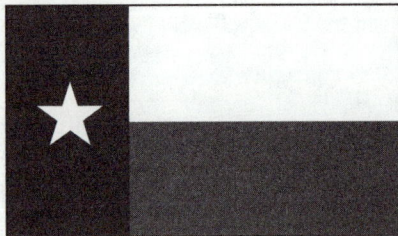

What type of angle is formed at each point of the lone star?

A Acute

B Obtuse

C Right

D Straight

2 How many cups are there in 1 gallon of water?

F 6

G 8

H 12

J 16

3 Which is the prime factorization of 36?

A $2 \times 2 \times 3 \times 2$

B $2^3 \times 3^2$

C $2^2 \times 3^3$

D $2^2 \times 3^2$

4 Mira, Anil, Emily, and Jason are playing a card game. The winner is the player who holds the most cards. Mira has 14 more cards than Emily. Emily has twice as many as Jason. Jason has 2 fewer cards than Anil. Anil has 8 cards. Who is the winner of the game?

F Anil

G Emily

H Jason

J Mira

GO

5 The table shows how many cans of dog food can be packed into cartons that are then shipped to supermarkets.

Cartons	Cans of Dog Food
1	48
2	96
3	144
4	192
5	240

Which formula describes the relationship between c, the number of cartons, and d, the number of cans of dog food that can fit in c cartons?

A $c = 48 \times d$

B $c = 48 + d$

C $d = 48 \times c$

D Not Here

6 Tara is making a square pattern using pennies. She makes each new step of the pattern by adding on pennies to the step before it. The first four steps are shown below.

1st Step **2nd Step** **3rd Step** **4th Step**

How many pennies must Tara add on to the 4th step to make the 5th step of the pattern?

F 5

G 9

H 10

J 11

GO▶

113

7 Rodney has dress shirts that are white, blue, tan, and yellow. He has a striped tie and a plaid tie. Which answer shows all the possible combinations of shirt and tie that Rodney can wear?

A

Shirt	Tie
White	Striped
Blue	Plaid
Tan	Striped
Yellow	Plaid
Blue	Striped
White	Plaid
Tan	Striped
Yellow	Plaid

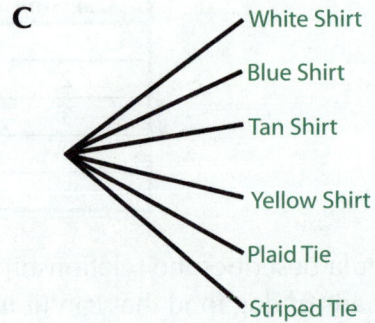

B

Shirt	Tie
White	Striped
White	Plaid
Blue	Striped
Blue	Plaid
Tan	Striped
Tan	Plaid
Yellow	Striped
Yellow	Plaid

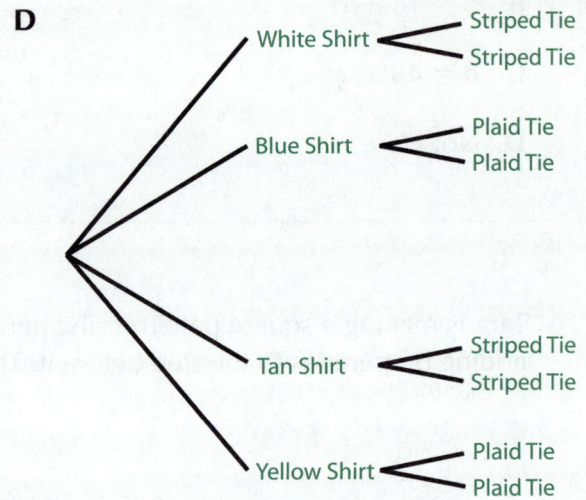

C

- White Shirt
- Blue Shirt
- Tan Shirt
- Yellow Shirt
- Plaid Tie
- Striped Tie

D

- White Shirt
  - Striped Tie
  - Striped Tie
- Blue Shirt
  - Plaid Tie
  - Plaid Tie
- Tan Shirt
  - Striped Tie
  - Striped Tie
- Yellow Shirt
  - Plaid Tie
  - Plaid Tie

8 Lana drew 2 circles. The diameter of the first circle is 6 cm. The radius of the second circle is twice the radius of the first circle. Which is the diameter of the second circle?

F 3 cm

G 6 cm

H 9 cm

J 12 cm

9 Which model best represents the inequality $\frac{1}{2} > \frac{1}{3}$?

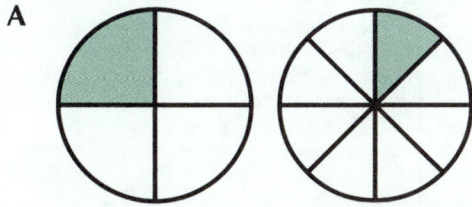

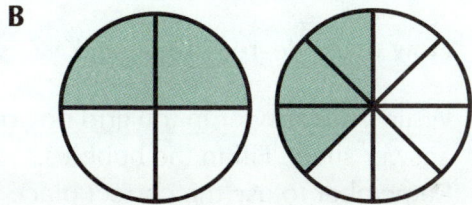

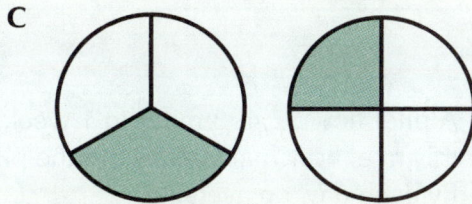

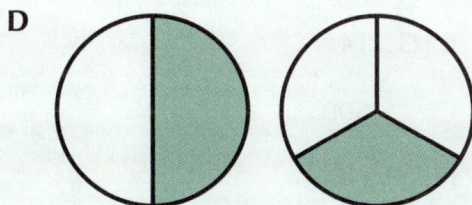

A

B

C

D

10 Nell needs to ship 7 gift packages to her friends. The postal service charges by weight. The lightest package weighs 1.5 pounds, and the heaviest package weighs 5 pounds. Which is a reasonable total weight of the packages?

F 13 lbs

G 25 lbs

H 35 lbs

J 45 lbs

11 During the 20th century, the city of Billoughie had fifteen mayors. The table below shows the number of years each of those mayors served in office.

8, 12, 4, 4, 1, 7, 4, 8, 4, 20, 8, 4, 8, 4, 4

What was the range in number of years served by mayors of Billoughie during the 20th century?

Write your answer in the grid on your answer sheet. Fill in the bubbles. Remember to use the correct place value.

GO➡

12 A company makes rubber bands that are $3\frac{1}{2}$ inches long. Their four types differ by width, as shown in the table.

Size	Width	Number per pound
A	$\frac{1}{2}$ in.	235
B	$\frac{1}{4}$ in.	460
C	$\frac{1}{8}$ in.	880
D	$\frac{3}{8}$ in.	335

How much greater is the width of the widest rubber band than that of the next widest rubber band?

A $\frac{1}{8}$ in.

B $\frac{1}{4}$ in.

C $\frac{1}{6}$ in.

D $\frac{3}{8}$ in.

13 Mario's long distance telephone plan costs him $9.95 per month plus $0.07 per minute for each call he makes. Mario estimates that he makes 10–20 minutes of long distance calls per day. Which is NOT a reasonable amount for Mario to expect to pay for one month?

F $32

G $40

H $46

J $54

14 *JKLM* is a rectangle.

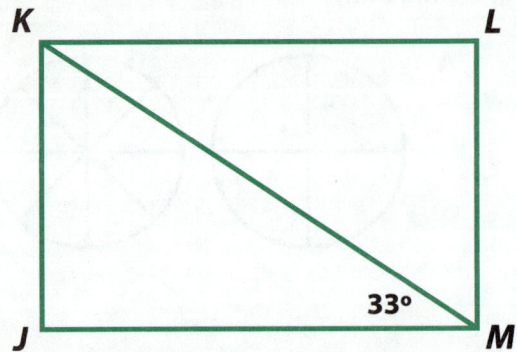

How many degrees are in ∠*JKM*?

Write your answer in the grid on your answer sheet. Fill in the bubbles. Remember to use the correct place value.

15 A pilot flew 22,498 miles in 1 week. At this rate, how many miles did the pilot fly each day, on average?

A 1,607

B 3,214

C 75,500

D 157,486

GO➤

116

16 What percent of the figure shown is shaded?

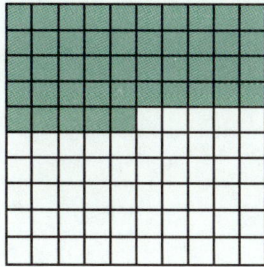

F 0.45%

G 4.5%

H 45%

J 4,500%

17 Which point on the number line below represents 3.4?

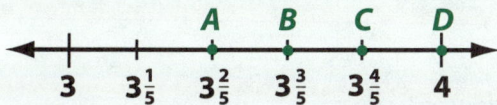

A Point *A*

B Point *B*

C Point *C*

D Point *D*

18 A sack contains twelve white, gray, and black socks, as shown below.

If one sock is chosen without looking, what is the probability that a white sock is NOT chosen?

F $\frac{6}{6}$

G $\frac{2}{1}$

H $\frac{1}{3}$

J $\frac{1}{2}$

GO ➡

19 Which ordered pair best represents point *T* on the coordinate grid below?

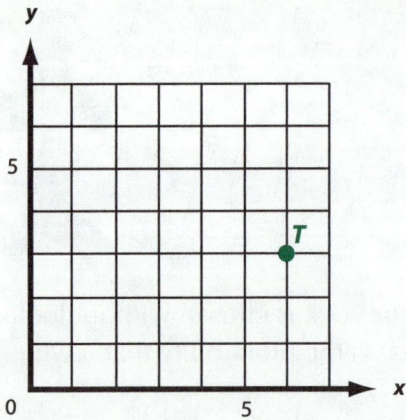

A (6, 2)

B (6, 3)

C (3, 6)

D (2, 6)

20 A sport utility vehicle weighs 4,960 pounds. How many tons is 4,960 pounds?

F 1.48 tons

G 2.48 tons

H 2.96 tons

J 4.96 tons

21 What is the measure of ∠*POR*, to the nearest degree?

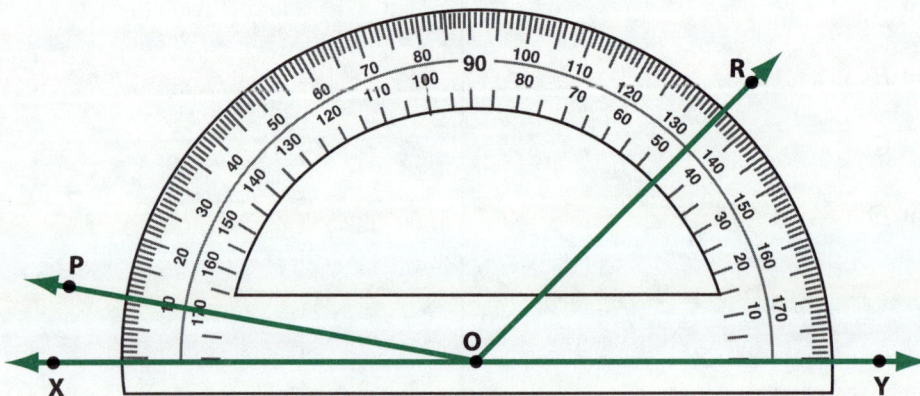

A 125°   **C** 145°

B 135°   **D** 170°

GO▶

22 A survey of 20 students asked, "How many times did you see a movie last month?" The bar graph below shows the results of the survey.

**Movie Survey:
How Many Times Did You See a Movie Last Month?**

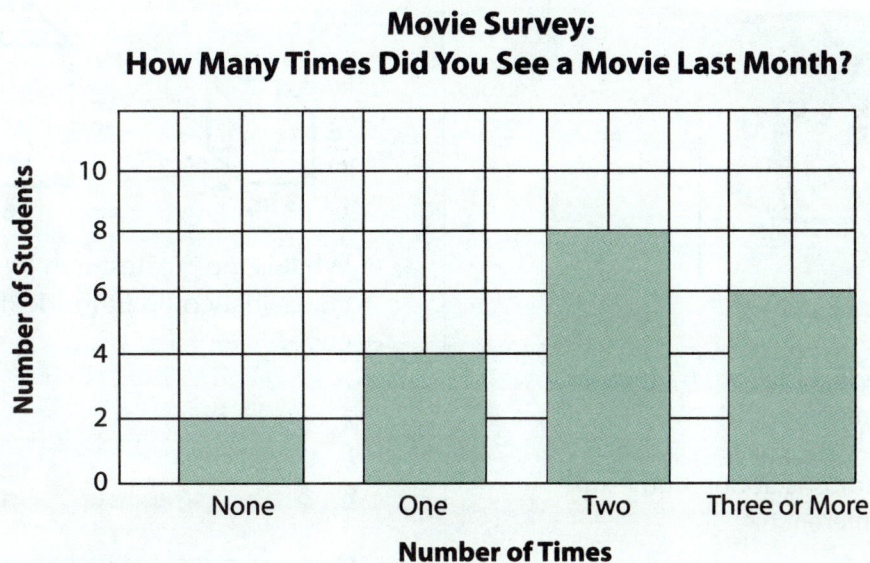

How many students in the survey did NOT see three or more movies?

F 18   **H** 9

G 14   **J** 7

---

23 Eva earns $50 per day plus $10 for each new customer she signs up. One week, Eva worked 5 days and signed up 18 new customers. Which equation could be used to find *s*, her salary for that week?

A $s = 5 \times (50 + 10) + 18$

B $s = (5 \times 50) + (18 \times 10)$

C $s = (5 \times 50) + 10 + 18$

D $s = (50 + 10) \times (5 + 18)$

24 Tim was hired to mow four lawns this week. The smallest lawn has an area of 1,200 square feet. The largest lawn has an area of 3,000 square feet. Which of the following could be the total area of the lawns Tim must mow this week?

F 4,800 square feet

G 6,100 square feet

H 8,100 square feet

J 10,500 square feet

GO➡

25 How is the radius of the top of a can of paint related to its circumference?

A The radius is about 6 times the circumference.

B The radius is about 3 times the circumference.

C The radius is about $\frac{1}{3}$ the circumference.

D The radius is about $\frac{1}{6}$ the circumference.

26 Hot sausage is sold in pieces that are each about 1 foot long. The price of a piece ranges from $6.25 to $7.50. Beverly is buying 9 pieces of hot sausage for a large party she is catering. Which is the best estimate of what Beverly should expect to spend for the sausage?

F Between $70 and $90

G Between $50 and $70

H Between $30 and $50

J Less than $30

27 The figures shown below are cubes.

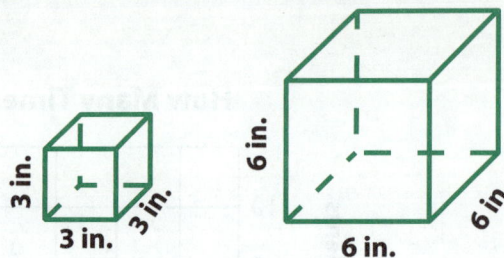

What is the greatest number of smaller cubes that could fit inside the larger cube?

A 8

B 6

C 4

D 2

28 Mr. Marks has 200 books in his library. Of those books, 75 are science fiction, 53 are mysteries, 38 are biographies, and 34 are nonfiction. Which ratio represents the number of science fiction books to the total number of books in his library?

F 3 to 8

G 17 to 100

H 19 to 100

J 53 to 100

GO

29 In March 2002, the price of iceberg lettuce rose greatly. The table below shows the average price of a head of lettuce at a store in Houston over a four-week period.

Week	1	2	3	4
Price per head	$1.29	$1.50	$1.89	$2.69

Which graph best represents the same data?

A Lettuce Prices Over Four Weeks

C Lettuce Prices Over Four Weeks

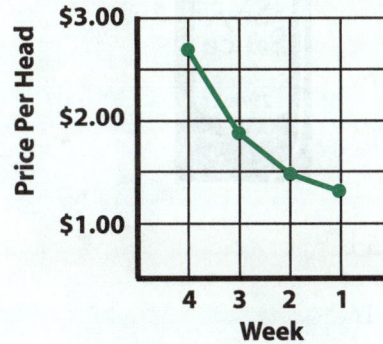

B Lettuce Prices Over Four Weeks

D Lettuce Prices Over Four Weeks

Stem	Leaf
12	9
15	0
18	9
26	9

30 Al's Music Mania is having a promotional drawing for a free recording. A customer will reach into a box and draw out a coupon for either a cassette or a compact disc of one of these four types of music: Classical, Rock, Rap, or Country & Western. If each type of coupon is equally likely to be selected, what is the probability of the customer selecting a coupon for a Rap compact disc?

F $\frac{1}{2}$ **H** $\frac{1}{8}$

G $\frac{1}{4}$ **J** $\frac{1}{16}$

GO➤

31 What is the capacity of the bottle of soy sauce below, in liters?

A 0.25 L

B 2.5 L

C 25 L

D Not Here

32 Samantha is buying pizzas for a group of 18 boys and 14 girls. She wants to buy two slices per child. One pizza costs $10. What other information must Samantha know before she can calculate how many pizzas to buy?

F The total cost of the pizzas

G The greatest number of slices any child wants to eat

H The number of slices in a pizza

J Number of adults

33 The numbers 0.7, 0.098, $\frac{3}{4}$, and $1\frac{1}{2}$ were placed on a number line.

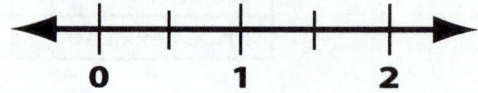

Which number was closest to 1?

A 0.7

B 0.098

C $\frac{3}{4}$

D $1\frac{1}{2}$

34 Which group contains fractions that are all equivalent to $\frac{3}{8}$?

F $\frac{6}{16}$, $\frac{9}{24}$, $\frac{12}{32}$

G $\frac{12}{24}$, $\frac{24}{32}$, $\frac{30}{40}$

H $\frac{6}{16}$, $\frac{6}{32}$, $\frac{24}{40}$

J $\frac{9}{16}$, $\frac{12}{24}$, $\frac{18}{32}$

GO ➤

35 The circle below has center *C* and a radius of 8 cm. Triangle *ABC* has a perimeter of 25 cm.

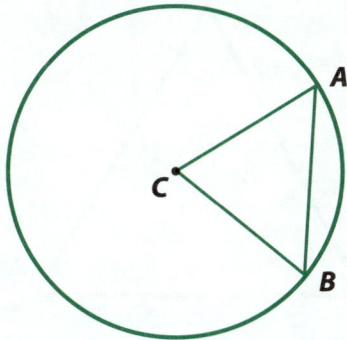

What can be concluded about the length of $\overline{AB}$?

A The length of $\overline{AB}$ is less than 8 cm.

B The length of $\overline{AB}$ equals 8 cm.

C The length of $\overline{AB}$ is greater than 8 cm and less than 17 cm.

D The length of $\overline{AB}$ equals 17 cm.

36 Look at the number pattern in the box.

> **9, 18, 27, 36, ...**

Which number sentence can be used to find *g*, the eleventh number in the pattern?

F $g = 9 \times 11$

G $g = 9 + 11$

H $g = 36 \times 11$

J $g = 36 + 11$

37 Emilia arrived at work at the time shown on the first clock below. She left work at the time shown on the second clock.

How long was Emilia at work?

A 6 hours 50 minutes

B 6 hours 10 minutes

C 5 hours 50 minutes

D Not Here

GO➡

123

38 A drawing of a stamp in actual size is shown below. Next to it is an enlargement of the stamp made for a catalog.

Original Stamp

28 mm

44 mm

3

Enlargement

35 mm

55 mm

What is the ratio of the dimensions of the enlarged stamp to the dimensions of the original stamp?

F 2 to 3   H 4 to 5

G 3 to 2   J 5 to 4

39 Janet is four times as old as her son, Juan. In five years, Juan will be fourteen years old. How old is Janet now?

Write your answer in the grid on your answer sheet. Fill in the bubbles. Remember to use the correct place value.

40 $\triangle ABC$ is an isosceles triangle in which side $\overline{AB}$ and side $\overline{AC}$ are congruent.

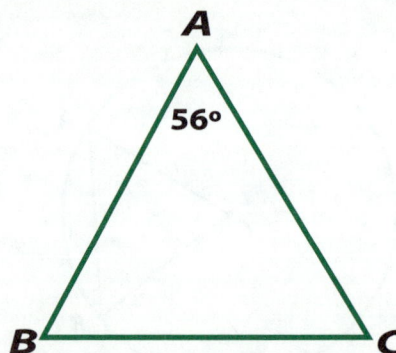

A

56°

B   C

What is the measure of $\angle B$?

A 52°

B 62°

C 64°

D 67°

41 A spinner is divided into 12 equal sections. There are 5 green sections, 4 red sections, and 3 blue sections. The pointer on the spinner is spun 36 times. Which proportion can be used to find G, the number of times that the pointer could be expected to land on a green section?

F $\dfrac{G}{12} = \dfrac{5}{36}$

G $\dfrac{5}{12} = \dfrac{G}{36}$

H $\dfrac{5}{12} = \dfrac{36}{G}$

J $\dfrac{12}{36} - 12 = \dfrac{5}{G}$

GO

42 When a coin is tossed, it lands on Heads or Tails. A coin is tossed three times. The list below shows some of the possible outcomes for the three tosses.

Some Possible Outcomes		
First Toss	**Second Toss**	**Third Toss**
Heads	Heads	Tails
Heads	Tails	Heads
Heads	Tails	Tails
Tails	Heads	Heads
Tails	Heads	Tails
Tails	Tails	Heads

How many more possible outcomes are there?

A 4

B 3

C 2

D 1

43 The temperature during a record-breaking cold spell was eight degrees below zero one morning. How is this temperature written?

F $\frac{0}{8}$

G $(\frac{0}{8})°$

H $8°$

J $-8°$

44 Which point best represents the ordered pair $(\frac{1}{2}, \frac{3}{4})$ on the coordinate grid below?

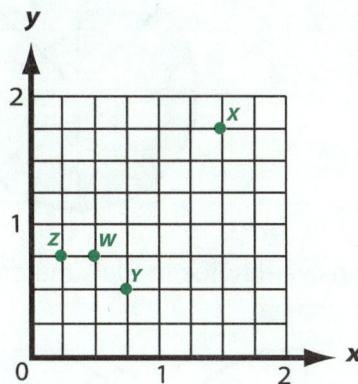

A Point W

B Point X

C Point Y

D Point Z

45 A group of scouts ordered two cakes. They ate $\frac{3}{4}$ of the first cake and $\frac{1}{2}$ of the second cake. Taylor drew the picture shown below to model the original two cakes.

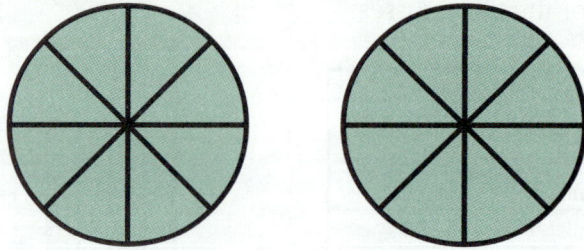

Which answer choice models the cake that was left over after the scouts ate?

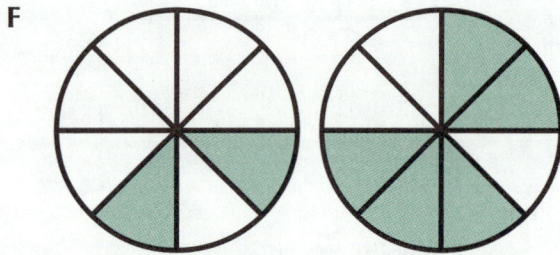

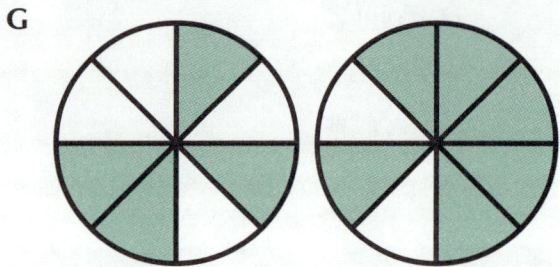

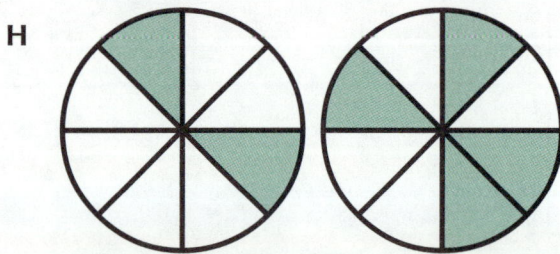

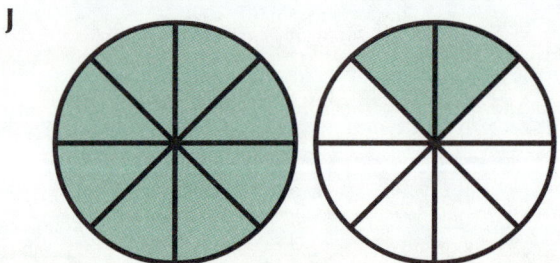

F

G

H

J

GO ➡

46 Look at the triangle below. Use the ruler on the Mathematics Chart to measure the perimeter of the figure in centimeters.

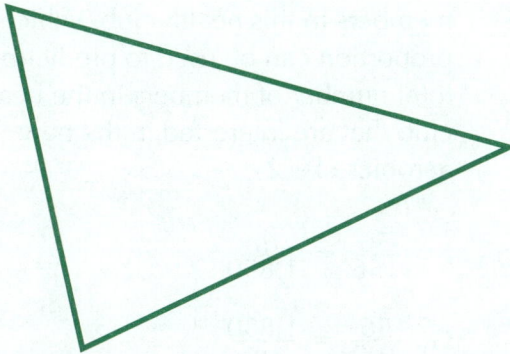

Which is the best estimate of the perimeter of the triangle?

A 20 cm

B 18 cm

C 16 cm

D 14 cm

47 Mariko bought four 8-ounce containers of yogurt. She handed the clerk a $5 bill and received $1.84 in change. Which equation could be used to find y, the cost of an 8-ounce container of yogurt?

F $y = 1.84 \div 4$

G $y = (5 + 1.84) - 4$

H $y = (5 - 1.84) \times 4$

J $y = (5 - 1.84) \div 4$

48 How many common factors do 16 and 18 have?

A 1

B 2

C 3

D Not Here

GO ➡️

49 ∠*A* in Δ*ABC* is a right angle. ∠*B* measures 51°. What is the measure of ∠*C*?

    F 39°

    G 40°

    H 49°

    J 51°

50 According to a newspaper article, a family is entitled to a tax credit if their family income is less than or equal to $50,000. If *f* stands for family income, which answer choice matches the condition for getting the tax credit?

    A $f \leq 50{,}000$

    B $f < 50{,}000$

    C $f > 50{,}000$

    D $f \geq 50{,}000$

51 A survey of 100 members of a health club finds that 56 are interested in a new aerobics class. There are 1,850 members in this health club. Which proportion can be used to predict *n*, the total number of members in the health club that are interested in the new aerobics class?

    F $\dfrac{56}{156} = \dfrac{n}{1{,}850}$

    G $\dfrac{56}{100} = \dfrac{1{,}850}{n}$

    H $\dfrac{56}{100} = \dfrac{n}{1{,}850}$

    J $\dfrac{44}{100} = \dfrac{1{,}850}{n}$

52 How many square centimeters is the area of the trapezoid shown below?

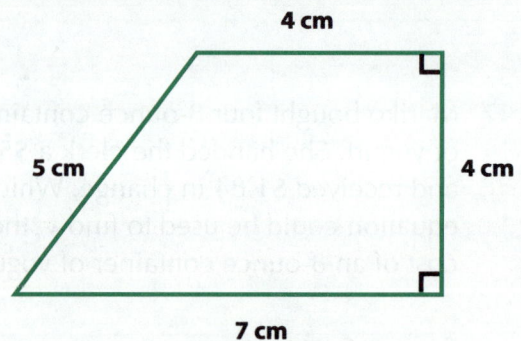

Write your answer in the grid on your answer sheet. Fill in the bubbles. Remember to use the correct place value.

GO ▶

53 A frame is used to enclose a work of art.

C

What type of angle does ∠*C* appear to be?

A Acute

B Obtuse

C Right

D Straight

54 A student is writing an article for her school newspaper on how four different classes sold magazine subscriptions. She wants to include a graph in her article that shows the number of subscriptions sold by each class. Which type of graph would be best to use?

F Bar graph

G Line graph

H Venn diagram

J Stem-and-leaf plot

55 The side lengths and volumes of some cubes are shown in the table below.

Volumes of Cubes	
Side Length (inches)	Volume (cubic inches)
2	8
3	27
4	64
5	125

Which expression can be used to find the volume, in cubic inches, of a cube whose side length is *n* inches?

A n^3

B $2n^2$

C $4n$

D $3n$

GO

56 Abraham Lincoln won the presidential election of 1860 to become the 16th President of the United States. The table below shows the percent of the popular vote that Lincoln and each of his three challengers received.

Candidate	Percent of Popular Vote
Abraham Lincoln	40%
Stephen Douglas	29%
John Breckinridge	18%
John Bell	13%

Which circle graph best displays the data shown in the table?

F   **Election of 1860—Popular Vote**

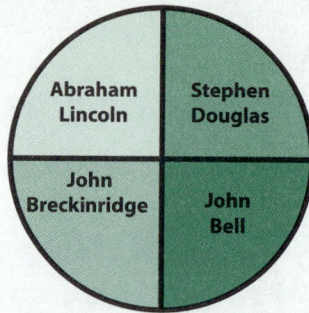

H   **Election of 1860—Popular Vote**

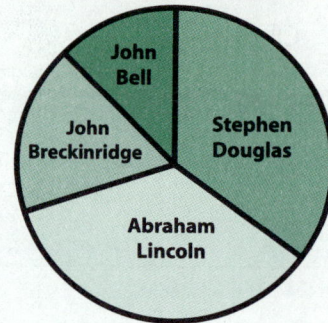

G   **Election of 1860—Popular Vote**

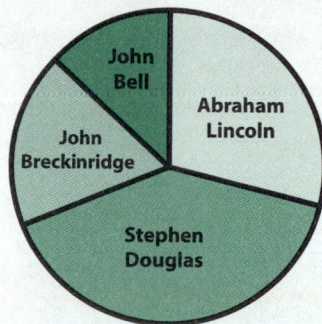

J   **Election of 1860—Popular Vote**

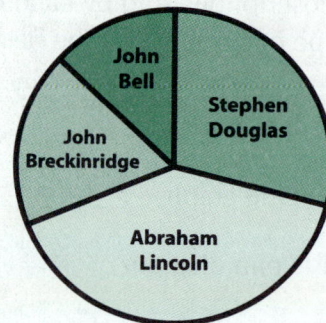

STOP

130

Modeled Instruction
Reading

Page 21

1	B	[Objective 1(6.9)(B)]
2	F	[Objective 2(6.12)(G)]
3	C	[Objective 2(6.12)(J)]
4	G	[Objective 4(6.10)(H)]

Page 22

5	D	[Objective 2(6.12)(F)]
6	J	[Objective 4(6.10)(H)]
7	C	[Objective 3(6.10)(L)]
8	G	[Objective 2(6.12)(F)]

Page 25

9	B	[Objective 3(6.10)(E)]
10	F	[Objective 4(6.12)(I)]
11	A	[Objective 3(6.10)(E)]
12	G	[Objective 3(6.10)(L)]

Page 26

13	B	[Objective 1(6.10)(G)]
14	H	[Objective 3(6.12)(A)]
15	D	[Objective 1(6.9)(B)]

Page 30

16	J	[Objective 1(6.10)(F)]
17	C	[Objective 1(6.9)(B)]
18	J	[Objective 4(6.10)(H)]
19	C	[Objective 2(6.12)(F)]

Page 31

20	G	[Objective 2(6.12)(F)]
21	D	[Objective 3(6.12)(A)]
22	H	[Objective 3(6.10)(L)]
23	A	[Objective 3(6.10)(E)]

Page 35

24	H	[Objective 1(6.10)(F)]
25	B	[Objective 2(6.12)(J)]
26	F	[Objective 2(6.12)(G)]
27	B	[Objective 4(6.10)(H)]

Page 36

28	F	[Objective 4(6.12)(K)]
29	C	[Objective 3(6.10)(E)]
30	F	[Objective 3(6.12)(C)]

Modeled Instruction
Writing

Page 39

1	A	[Objective 6(7.16)(B)]
2	J	[Objective 6(7.16)(F)]
3	A	[Objective 6(7.18)(H)]
4	H	[Objective 4(7.17)(B)]

Page 40

5	D	[Objective 3(7.18)(C)]
6	H	[Objective 4(7.17)(B)]
7	D	[Objective 6(7.18)(H)]
8	J	[Objective 4(7.17)(A)]

Page 41

Answers will vary, but all students should explain the importance of building relationships with people in the community.
[Objectives 1 and 2/All Expectations]

Test
Reading

Page 50

1	C	[Objective 4(6.12)(I)]
2	G	[Objective 1(6.9)(B)]
3	D	[Objective 3(6.12)(H)]

Page 51

4	F	[Objective 2(6.12)(J)]
5	D	[Objective 4(6.12)(K)]
6	H	[Objective 1(6.10)(G)]

Page 52

7	A	[Objective 2(6.12)(F)]
8	H	[Objective 2(6.12)(F)]
9	D	[Objective 3(6.10)(L)]

Page 56

10	H	[Objective 2(6.12)(F)]
11	B	[Objective 1(6.10)(F)]
12	F	[Objective 2(6.12)(F)]
13	D	[Objective 2(6.12)(J)]

Page 57

14	G	[Objective 1(6.10)(F)]
15	C	[Objective 1(6.10)(G)]
16	F	[Objective 2(6.12)(F)]
17	C	[Objective 3(6.10)(L)]

Page 58

18	J	[Objective 4(6.12)(I)]
19	A	[Objective 3(6.12)(A)]
20	J	[Objective 4(6.11)(D)]
21	B	[Objective 3(6.12)(C)]

Page 61

| 22 | H | [Objective 4(6.10)(H)] |
| 23 | A | [Objective 3(6.10)(E)] |

Page 62

24	H	[Objective 4(6.10)(H)]
25	D	[Objective 1(6.9)(B)]
26	H	[Objective 1(6.10)(F)]
27	B	[Objective 4(6.10)(H)]
28	F	[Objective 4(6.12)(I)]

Page 63

29	C	[Objective 3(6.10)(L)]
30	F	[Objective 3(6.10)(E)]
31	D	[Objective 1(6.10)(F)]

Page 67

| 32 | F | [Objective 1(6.9)(B)] |
| 33 | C | [Objective 4(6.10)(H)] |

Page 68

34	F	[Objective 2(6.12)(G)]
35	B	[Objective 2(6.12)(F)]
36	H	[Objective 1(6.9)(F)]
37	D	[Objective 4(6.12)(K)]

Page 69

38	G	[Objective 2(6.12)(F)]
39	D	[Objective 4(6.10)(J)]
40	H	[Objective 4(6.12)(I)]

Test
Writing

Page 70

| S-1 | C | [Objective 5(7.17)(F)] |
| S-2 | F | [Objective 5(7.17)(D)] |

Page 72

1	B	[Objective 5(7.17)(C)]
2	J	[Objective 5(7.18)(H)]
3	D	[Objective 4(7.17)(B)]
4	H	[Objective 5(7.17)(C)]
5	B	[Objective 3(7.18)(C)]

Page 73

6	J	[Objective 4(7.17)(B)]
7	C	[Objective 5(7.17)(C)]
8	J	[Objective 5(7.18)(E)]

Page 76

9	C	[Objective 4(7.17)(B)]
10	F	[Objective 4(7.18)(E)]
11	B	[Objective 6(7.16)(D)]
12	F	[Objective 5(7.17)(C)]
13	C	[Objective 6(7.16)(B)]

Page 77

14	J	[Objective 3(7.18)(D)]
15	A	[Objective 5(7.17)(D)]
16	J	[Objective 3(7.18)(C)]

Page 78

Answers will vary, but all students should describe a time when they made an important decision and relate the consequences of that decision.
[Objectives 1 and 2/All Expectations]

Modeled Instruction Mathematics

OBJECTIVE 1

Page 92

1   **C**   [Objective 1 (6.2)(C)]

2   **F**   [Objective 1 (6.1)(A)]

Page 93

3   **D**   [Objective 1 (6.1)(E)]

4   **G**   [Objective 1 (6.1)(D)]

5   **D**   [Objective 1 (6.2)(A)]

Page 94

6   **43.5**   [Objective 1 (6.2)(B)]

OBJECTIVE 2

Page 95

1   **C**   [Objective 2 (6.4)(A)]

2   **247**   [Objective 2 (6.3)(C)]

Page 96

3   **G**   [Objective 2 (6.4)(B)]

Page 97

4   **B**   [Objective 2 (6.3)(A)]

5   **F**   [Objective 2 (6.5)(A)]

OBJECTIVE 3

Page 98

1   **60**   [Objective 3 (6.6)(B)]

Page 99

2   **C**   [Objective 3 (6.6)(C)]

3   **F**   [Objective 3 (6.7)(A)]

Page 100

4   **B**   [Objective 3 (6.6)(A)]

5   **J**   [Objective 3 (6.6)(B)]

OBJECTIVE 4

Page 101

1   **B**   [Objective 4 (6.8)(C)]

2   **J**   [Objective 4 (6.8)(B)]

Page 102

3   **C**   [Objective 4 (6.8)(B)]

4   **F**   [Objective 4 (6.8)(D)]

5   **336**   [Objective 4 (6.8)(D)]

Page 103

6   **C**   [Objective 4 (6.8)(A)]

OBJECTIVE 5

Page 104

1   **A**   [Objective 5 (6.10)(D)]

2   **G**   [Objective 5 (6.9)(B)]

Page 105

3   **D**   [Objective 5 (6.9)(A)]

4   **17**   [Objective 5 (6.10)(B)]

Page 106

5   **H**   [Objective 5 (6.10)(C)]

OBJECTIVE 6

Page 107

1   **25**   [Objective 6 (6.13)(A)]

Page 108

2   **D**   [Objective 6 (6.11)(B)]

3   **F**   [Objective 6 (6.11)(A)]

4   **C**   [Objective 6 (6.12)(A)]

Page 109

5   **G**   [Objective 6 (6.11)(C)]

Test
Mathematics

Page 111

| Sample A | C | Objective 2 (6.3)(B) |
| Sample B | 0.6 | Objective 5 (6.9)(B) |

Page 112

1	A	[Objective 3 (6.6)(A)]
2	J	[Objective 4 (6.8)(D)]
3	D	[Objective 1 (6.1)(D)]
4	J	[Objective 6 (6.11)(C)]

Page 113

| 5 | C | [Objective 2 (6.4)(A)] |
| 6 | G | [Objective 6 (6.13)(A)] |

Page 114

| 7 | B | [Objective 5 (6.9)(A)] |
| 8 | J | [Objective 3 (6.6)(C)] |

Page 115

9	D	[Objective 6 (6.12)(A)]
10	G	[Objective 4 (6.8)(A)]
11	19	[Objective 5 (6.10)(B)]

Page 116

12	A	[Objective 1 (6.2)(B)]
13	J	[Objective 6 (6.11)(A)]
14	57	[Objective 3 (6.6)(B)]
15	B	[Objective 1 (6.2)(C)]

Page 117

16	H	[Objective 2 (6.3)(B)]
17	A	[Objective 1 (6.1)(B)]
18	J	[Objective 5 (6.9)(B)]

Page 118

19	B	[Objective 3 (6.7)(A)]
20	G	[Objective 4 (6.8)(D)]
21	A	[Objective 4 (6.8)(C)]

Page 119

22	G	[Objective 5 (6.10)(D)]
23	B	[Objective 2 (6.5)(A)]
24	H	[Objective 4 (6.8)(A)]

Page 120

25	D	[Objective 3 (6.6)(C)]
26	G	[Objective 1 (6.2)(D)]
27	A	[Objective 6 (6.13)(B)]
28	F	[Objective 2 (6.3)(A)]

Page 121

| 29 | B | [Objective 5 (6.10)(A)] |
| 30 | H | [Objective 5 (6.9)(B)] |

Page 122

31	A	[Objective 4 (6.8)(D)]
32	H	[Objective 6 (6.11)(B)]
33	C	[Objective 1 (6.1)(A)]
34	F	[Objective 1 (6.1)(B)]

Page 123

35	C	[Objective 6 (6.13)(B)]
36	F	[Objective 2 (6.4)(A)]
37	C	[Objective 4 (6.8)(B)]

Page 124

38	J	[Objective 2 (6.3)(A)]
39	36	[Objective 6 (6.11)(C)]
40	B	[Objective 3 (6.6)(B)]
41	G	[Objective 2 (6.3)(C)]

Page 125

42	C	[Objective 5 (6.9)(A)]
43	J	[Objective 1 (6.1)(C)]
44	A	[Objective 3 (6.7)(A)]

Page 126

| 45 | H | [Objective 1 (6.2)(A)] |

Page 127

46	B	[Objective 4 (6.8)(A)]
47	J	[Objective 2 (6.5)(A)]
48	B	[Objective 1 (6.1)(E)]

Page 128

49	F	[Objective 3 (6.6)(B)]
50	A	[Objective 6 (6.12)(A)]
51	H	[Objective 2 (6.3)(C)]
52	22	[Objective 4 (6.8)(B)]

Page 129

53	C	[Objective 3 (6.6)(A)]
54	F	[Objective 5 (6.10)(A)]
55	A	[Objective 2 (6.4)(B)]

Page 130

| 56 | J | [Objective 5 (6.10)(C)] |

READING

OBJECTIVE 1	The student will demonstrate a basic understanding of culturally diverse written texts.
(6.9)	1 [Expectation (B)]; 15 [Expectation (B)]; 17 [Expectation (B)]
(6.10)	13 [Expectation (G)]; 16 [Expectation (F)]; 24 [Expectation (F)]
OBJECTIVE 2	**The student will apply knowledge of literary elements to understand culturally diverse written texts.**
(6.12)	2 [Expectation (G)]; 3 [Expectation (J)]; 5 [Expectation (F)]; 8 [Expectation (F)]; 19 [Expectation (F)]; 20 [Expectation (F)]; 25 [Expectation (J)]; 26 [Expectation (G)]
OBJECTIVE 3	**The student will use a variety of strategies to analyze culturally diverse written texts.**
(6.10)	7 [Expectation (L)]; 9 [Expectation (E)]; 11 [Expectation (E)]; 12 [Expectation (L)]; 22 [Expectation (L)]; 23 [Expectation (E)]; 29 [Expectation (E)]
(6.12)	14 [Expectation (A)]; 21 [Expectation (A)]; 30 [Expectation (C)]
OBJECTIVE 4	**The student will apply critical-thinking skills to analyze culturally diverse written texts.**
(6.10)	4 [Expectation (H)]; 6 [Expectation (H)]; 18 [Expectation (H)]; 27 [Expectation (H)]
(6.11)	
(6.12)	10 [Expectation (I)]; 28 [Expectation (K)]

WRITING

OBJECTIVE 1	The student will, within a given context, produce an effective composition for a specific purpose.
(7.15)	Written Composition
(7.16)	Written Composition
(7.18)	Written Composition
OBJECTIVE 2	**The student will produce a piece of writing that demonstrates a command of the conventions of spelling, capitalization, punctuation, grammar, usage, and sentence structure.**
(7.16)	Written Composition
(7.17)	Written Composition
(7.18)	Written Composition
OBJECTIVE 3	**The student will recognize appropriate organization of ideas in written text.**
(7.18)	5 [Expectation (C)]
OBJECTIVE 4	**The student will recognize correct and effective sentence construction in written text.**
(7.17)	4 [Expectation (B)]; 6 [Expectation (B)]; 8 [Expectation (A)]
(7.18)	
OBJECTIVE 5	**The student will recognize standard usage and appropriate word choice in written text.**
(7.17)	
(7.18)	
OBJECTIVE 6	**The student will proofread for correct punctuation, capitalization, and spelling in written text.**
(7.16)	1 [Expectation (B)]; 2 [Expectation (F)]
(7.17)	
(7.18)	3 [Expectation (H)]; 7 [Expectation (H)]

Correlation of TAKS Objectives for Reading and Writing Tests

READING

OBJECTIVE 1	The student will demonstrate a basic understanding of culturally diverse written texts.
(6.9)	2 [Expectation (B)]; 25 [Expectation (B)]; 32 [Expectation (B)]; 36 [Expectation (F)]
(6.10)	6 [Expectation (G)]; 11 [Expectation (F)]; 14 [Expectation (F)]; 15 [Expectation (G)]; 26 [Expectation (F)]; 31 [Expectation (F)]
OBJECTIVE 2	**The student will apply knowledge of literary elements to understand culturally diverse written texts.**
(6.12)	4 [Expectation (J)]; 7 [Expectation (F)]; 8 [Expectation (F)]; 10 [Expectation (F)]; 12 [Expectation (F)]; 13 [Expectation (J)]; 16 [Expectation (F)]; 34 [Expectation (G)]; 35 [Expectation (F)]; 38 [Expectation (F)]
OBJECTIVE 3	**The student will use a variety of strategies to analyze culturally diverse written texts.**
(6.10)	9 [Expectation (L)]; 17 [Expectation (L)]; 23 [Expectation (E)]; 29 [Expectation (L)]; 30 [Expectation (E)]
(6.12)	3 [Expectation (H)]; 19 [Expectation (A)]; 21 [Expectation (C)]
OBJECTIVE 4	**The student will apply critical-thinking skills to analyze culturally diverse written texts.**
(6.10)	22 [Expectation (H)]; 24 [Expectation (H)]; 27 [Expectation (H)]; 33 [Expectation (H)]; 39 [Expectation (J)]
(6.11)	20 [Expectation (D)]
(6.12)	1 [Expectation (I)]; 5 [Expectation (K)]; 18 [Expectation (I)]; 28 [Expectation (I)]; 37 [Expectation (K)]; 40 [Expectation (I)]

WRITING

OBJECTIVE 1	The student will, within a given context, produce an effective composition for a specific purpose.
(7.15)	Written Composition
(7.16)	Written Composition
(7.18)	Written Composition
OBJECTIVE 2	**The student will produce a piece of writing that demonstrates a command of the conventions of spelling, capitalization, punctuation, grammar, usage, and sentence structure.**
(7.16)	Written Composition
(7.17)	Written Composition
(7.18)	Written Composition
OBJECTIVE 3	**The student will recognize appropriate organization of ideas in written text.**
(7.18)	5 [Expectation (C)]; 14 [Expectation (D)]; 16 [Expectation (C)]
OBJECTIVE 4	**The student will recognize correct and effective sentence construction in written text.**
(7.17)	3 [Expectation (B)]; 6 [Expectation (B)]; 9 [Expectation (B)]
(7.18)	10 [Expectation (E)]
OBJECTIVE 5	**The student will recognize standard usage and appropriate word choice in written text.**
(7.17)	S-1 [Expectation (F)]; S-2 [Expectation (D)]; 1 [Expectation (C)]; 4 [Expectation (C)]; 7 [Expectation (C)]; 12 [Expectation (C)]; 15 [Expectation (D)]
(7.18)	2 [Expectation (H)]; 8 [Expectation (E)]
OBJECTIVE 6	**The student will proofread for correct punctuation, capitalization, and spelling in written text.**
(7.16)	11 [Expectation (D)]; 13 [Expectation (B)]
(7.17)	
(7.18)	

Correlation of TAKS Objectives for Mathematics Modeled Instruction

OBJECTIVE 1 [pp. 92–94]	**The student will demonstrate an understanding of numbers, operations, and quantitative reasoning.**
(6.1) **(6.2)**	2 [Expectation (A)]; 3 [Expectation (E)]; 4 [Expectation (D)] 1 [Expectation (C)]; 5 [Expectation (A)]; 6 [Expectation (B)]
OBJECTIVE 2 [pp. 95–97]	**The student will demonstrate an understanding of patterns, relationships, and algebraic reasoning.**
(6.3) **(6.4)** **(6.5)**	2 [Expectation (C)]; 4 [Expectation (A)] 1 [Expectation (A)]; 3 [Expectation (B)] 5 [Expectation (A)]
OBJECTIVE 3 [pp. 98–100]	**The student will demonstrate an understanding of geometry and spatial reasoning.**
(6.6) **(6.7)**	1 [Expectation (B)]; 2 [Expectation (C)]; 4 [Expectation (A)]; 5 [Expectation (B)] 3 [Expectation (A)]
OBJECTIVE 4 [pp. 101–103]	**The student will demonstrate an understanding of the concepts and uses of measurement.**
(6.8)	1 [Expectation (C)]; 2 [Expectation (B)]; 3 [Expectation (B)]; 4 [Expectation (D)]; 5 [Expectation (D)]; 6 [Expectation (A)]
OBJECTIVE 5 [pp. 104–106]	**The student will demonstrate an understanding of probability and statistics.**
(6.9) **(6.10)**	2 [Expectation (B)]; 3 [Expectation (A)] 1 [Expectation (D)]; 4 [Expectation (B)]; 5 [Expectation (C)]
OBJECTIVE 6 [pp. 107–109]	**The student will demonstrate an understanding of the mathematical processes and tools used in problem solving.**
(6.11) **(6.12)** **(6.13)**	2 [Expectation (B)]; 3 [Expectation (A)]; 5 [Expectation (C)] 4 [Expectation (A)] 1 [Expectation (A)]

Correlation of TAKS Objectives for Mathematics Test

OBJECTIVE 1	The student will demonstrate an understanding of numbers, operations, and quantitative reasoning.
(6.1)	3 [Expectation (D)]; 17 [Expectation (B)]; 33 [Expectation (A)]; 34 [Expectation (B)]; 43 [Expectation (C)]; 48 [Expectation (E)]
(6.2)	12 [Expectation (B)]; 15 [Expectation (C)]; 26 [Expectation (D)]; 45 [Expectation (A)]
OBJECTIVE 2	**The student will demonstrate an understanding of patterns, relationships, and algebraic reasoning.**
(6.3)	SAMPLE A [Expectation (B)]; 16 [Expectation (B)]; 28 [Expectation (A)]; 38 [Expectation (A)]; 41 [Expectation (C)]; 51 [Expectation (C)]
(6.4)	5 [Expectation (A)]; 36 [Expectation (A)]; 55 [Expectation (B)]
(6.5)	23 [Expectation (A)]; 47 [Expectation (A)]
OBJECTIVE 3	**The student will demonstrate an understanding of geometry and spatial reasoning.**
(6.6)	1 [Expectation (A)]; 8 [Expectation (C)]; 14 [Expectation (B)]; 25 [Expectation (C)]; 40 [Expectation (B)]; 49 [Expectation (B)]; 53 [Expectation (A)]
(6.7)	19 [Expectation (A)]; 44 [Expectation (A)]
OBJECTIVE 4	**The student will demonstrate an understanding of the concepts and uses of measurement.**
(6.8)	2 [Expectation (D)]; 10 [Expectation (A)]; 20 [Expectation (D)]; 21 [Expectation (C)]; 24 [Expectation (A)]; 31 [Expectation (D)]; 37 [Expectation (B)]; 46 [Expectation (A)]; 52 [Expectation (B)]
OBJECTIVE 5	**The student will demonstrate an understanding of probability and statistics.**
(6.9)	SAMPLE B [Expectation (B)]; 7 [Expectation (A)]; 18 [Expectation (B)]; 30 [Expectation (B)]; 42 [Expectation (A)]
(6.10)	11 [Expectation (B)]; 22 [Expectation (D)]; 29 [Expectation (A)]; 54 [Expectation (A)]; 56 [Expectation (C)]
OBJECTIVE 6	**The student will demonstrate an understanding of the mathematical processes and tools used in problem solving.**
(6.11)	4 [Expectation (C)]; 13 [Expectation (A)]; 32 [Expectation (B)]; 39 [Expectation (C)]
(6.12)	9 [Expectation (A)]; 50 [Expectation (A)]
(6.13)	6 [Expectation (A)]; 27 [Expectation (B)]; 35 [Expectation (B)]

Evaluation Chart Information

An evaluation chart has been provided for your convenience on page 140. The purpose of this evaluation chart is to map your child's performance on the Test sections of this book. Using this chart will give you a good view of your child's strengths and weaknesses in terms of the TAKS objectives. Using this chart can help you pinpoint areas where your child needs extra practice.

Student Name: Sally Student

Question	Objective 1	Objective 2	Objective 3	Objective 4	Objective 5	Objective 6
1		1				
2			1			
3	1					
4					1	
5		1				
6					1	
7				0		
8		0				
9						0
10			1			
11				0		
12	0					
13					1	
14		0				
15	0					
16		1				
17	1					
18				0		
19		0				
20			1			
21			1			
22				1		
23	0					
24			1			
25		1				
26	1					
27						1
28		1				
29					0	

(continue on right column)

Question	Objective 1	Objective 2	Objective 3	Objective 4	Objective 5	Objective 6
30						1
31			1			
32						1
33	1					
34	0					
35					1	
36		1				
37			1			
38	1					
39						1
40		0				
41	1					
42				0		
43	1					
44			0			
45	1					
46				0		
47	1					
48	1					
49				1		
50						1
51	0					
52				1		
53		0				
54					0	
55	0					
56						1
Totals	7/10	7/10	3/9	8/9	3/9	8/9

Weak
Objectives: 3, 5

Strong
Objectives: 4, 6

An example of the chart is shown at left. Notice how the chart is filled in:

1) A **1** is written in every box that corresponds to an answer that was **correct** in the Test section.

2) A **0** is written in every box that corresponds to an answer that was **incorrect** in the Test section.

3) All of the 1's in each objective column are added up. That total is then placed as a numerator in the **Totals** row on the chart. For instance, Sally Student got 8 out of 9 items correct for Objective 6.

4) After reviewing the **Totals** row, Sally Student's weak and strong objectives are listed. The parent may now provide more practice in those areas.

Use the chart on the following page to map your child's performance.

Evaluation Chart

READING

Question	OBJECTIVE 1	OBJECTIVE 2	OBJECTIVE 3	OBJECTIVE 4
1				
2				
3				
4				
5				
6				
7				
8				
9				
10				
11				
12				
13				
14				
15				
16				
17				
18				
19				
20				
21				
22				
23				
24				
25				
26				
27				
28				
29				
30				
31				
32				
33				
34				
35				
36				
37				
38				
39				
40				
Totals	10	10	8	12

Weak Objectives: _____

Strong Objectives: _____

WRITING

Question	OBJECTIVE 1	OBJECTIVE 2	OBJECTIVE 3	OBJECTIVE 4	OBJECTIVE 5	OBJECTIVE 6
1						
2						
3						
4						
5						
6						
7						
8						
9						
10						
11						
12						
13						
14						
15						
16						
Totals			3	4	7	2

* The Written Composition should be scored separately by the rubric on page 7.

NOTE: Objectives 1 and 2 apply to the Written Composition only.

MATHEMATICS

Question	Objective 1	Objective 2	Objective 3	Objective 4	Objective 5	Objective 6
1						
2						
3						
4						
5						
6						
7						
8						
9						
10						
11						
12						
13						
14						
15						
16						
17						
18						
19						
20						
21						
22						
23						
24						
25						
26						
27						
28						
29						

(continue on right column)

Question	Objective 1	Objective 2	Objective 3	Objective 4	Objective 5	Objective 6
30						
31						
32						
33						
34						
35						
36						
37						
38						
39						
40						
41						
42						
43						
44						
45						
46						
47						
48						
49						
50						
51						
52						
53						
54						
55						
56						
Totals	10	10	9	9	9	9

Weak Objectives: _____

Strong Objectives: _____

Reading and Writing Test Answer Sheet

STUDENT'S NAME			SCHOOL:
LAST	FIRST	MI	TEACHER:

FEMALE ○   MALE ○

BIRTH DATE

MONTH	DAY		YEAR	
Jan ○	⓪	⓪	⑦	⓪
Feb ○	①	①	⑧	①
Mar ○	②	②	⑨	②
Apr ○	③	③	⓪	③
May ○		④		④
Jun ○		⑤		⑤
Jul ○		⑥		⑥
Aug ○		⑦		⑦
Sep ○		⑧		⑧
Oct ○		⑨		⑨
Nov ○				
Dec ○				

GRADE ④ ⑤ ⑥ ⑦ ⑧

TAKS READING AND WRITING GRADE 6

(Name grid columns with bubbles A–Z for LAST, FIRST, and MI.)

READING TEST

1 Ⓐ Ⓑ Ⓒ Ⓓ	8 Ⓕ Ⓖ Ⓗ Ⓙ	15 Ⓐ Ⓑ Ⓒ Ⓓ	22 Ⓕ Ⓖ Ⓗ Ⓙ	29 Ⓐ Ⓑ Ⓒ Ⓓ	36 Ⓕ Ⓖ Ⓗ Ⓙ
2 Ⓕ Ⓖ Ⓗ Ⓙ	9 Ⓐ Ⓑ Ⓒ Ⓓ	16 Ⓕ Ⓖ Ⓗ Ⓙ	23 Ⓐ Ⓑ Ⓒ Ⓓ	30 Ⓕ Ⓖ Ⓗ Ⓙ	37 Ⓐ Ⓑ Ⓒ Ⓓ
3 Ⓐ Ⓑ Ⓒ Ⓓ	10 Ⓕ Ⓖ Ⓗ Ⓙ	17 Ⓐ Ⓑ Ⓒ Ⓓ	24 Ⓕ Ⓖ Ⓗ Ⓙ	31 Ⓐ Ⓑ Ⓒ Ⓓ	38 Ⓕ Ⓖ Ⓗ Ⓙ
4 Ⓕ Ⓖ Ⓗ Ⓙ	11 Ⓐ Ⓑ Ⓒ Ⓓ	18 Ⓕ Ⓖ Ⓗ Ⓙ	25 Ⓐ Ⓑ Ⓒ Ⓓ	32 Ⓕ Ⓖ Ⓗ Ⓙ	39 Ⓐ Ⓑ Ⓒ Ⓓ
5 Ⓐ Ⓑ Ⓒ Ⓓ	12 Ⓕ Ⓖ Ⓗ Ⓙ	19 Ⓐ Ⓑ Ⓒ Ⓓ	26 Ⓕ Ⓖ Ⓗ Ⓙ	33 Ⓐ Ⓑ Ⓒ Ⓓ	40 Ⓕ Ⓖ Ⓗ Ⓙ
6 Ⓕ Ⓖ Ⓗ Ⓙ	13 Ⓐ Ⓑ Ⓒ Ⓓ	20 Ⓕ Ⓖ Ⓗ Ⓙ	27 Ⓐ Ⓑ Ⓒ Ⓓ	34 Ⓕ Ⓖ Ⓗ Ⓙ	
7 Ⓐ Ⓑ Ⓒ Ⓓ	14 Ⓕ Ⓖ Ⓗ Ⓙ	21 Ⓐ Ⓑ Ⓒ Ⓓ	28 Ⓕ Ⓖ Ⓗ Ⓙ	35 Ⓐ Ⓑ Ⓒ Ⓓ	

WRITING TEST

S-1 Ⓐ Ⓑ Ⓒ Ⓓ	2 Ⓕ Ⓖ Ⓗ Ⓙ	5 Ⓐ Ⓑ Ⓒ Ⓓ	8 Ⓕ Ⓖ Ⓗ Ⓙ	11 Ⓐ Ⓑ Ⓒ Ⓓ	14 Ⓕ Ⓖ Ⓗ Ⓙ
S-2 Ⓕ Ⓖ Ⓗ Ⓙ	3 Ⓐ Ⓑ Ⓒ Ⓓ	6 Ⓕ Ⓖ Ⓗ Ⓙ	9 Ⓐ Ⓑ Ⓒ Ⓓ	12 Ⓕ Ⓖ Ⓗ Ⓙ	15 Ⓐ Ⓑ Ⓒ Ⓓ
1 Ⓐ Ⓑ Ⓒ Ⓓ	4 Ⓕ Ⓖ Ⓗ Ⓙ	7 Ⓐ Ⓑ Ⓒ Ⓓ	10 Ⓕ Ⓖ Ⓗ Ⓙ	13 Ⓐ Ⓑ Ⓒ Ⓓ	16 Ⓕ Ⓖ Ⓗ Ⓙ

Mathematics Test Answer Sheet

Student's Name:

LAST | FIRST | MI

School: | **Teacher:**

Female ○ **Male** ○ | **Grade:** ⑤ ⑥ ⑦ ⑧

SA Ⓐ Ⓑ Ⓒ Ⓓ

SB

1 Ⓐ Ⓑ Ⓒ Ⓓ
2 Ⓕ Ⓖ Ⓗ Ⓙ
3 Ⓐ Ⓑ Ⓒ Ⓓ
4 Ⓕ Ⓖ Ⓗ Ⓙ
5 Ⓐ Ⓑ Ⓒ Ⓓ
6 Ⓕ Ⓖ Ⓗ Ⓙ
7 Ⓐ Ⓑ Ⓒ Ⓓ
8 Ⓕ Ⓖ Ⓗ Ⓙ
9 Ⓐ Ⓑ Ⓒ Ⓓ
10 Ⓕ Ⓖ Ⓗ Ⓙ

11 (grid)

12 Ⓐ Ⓑ Ⓒ Ⓓ
13 Ⓕ Ⓖ Ⓗ Ⓙ

14 (grid)

15 Ⓐ Ⓑ Ⓒ Ⓓ
16 Ⓕ Ⓖ Ⓗ Ⓙ
17 Ⓐ Ⓑ Ⓒ Ⓓ
18 Ⓕ Ⓖ Ⓗ Ⓙ
19 Ⓐ Ⓑ Ⓒ Ⓓ
20 Ⓕ Ⓖ Ⓗ Ⓙ
21 Ⓐ Ⓑ Ⓒ Ⓓ
22 Ⓕ Ⓖ Ⓗ Ⓙ
23 Ⓐ Ⓑ Ⓒ Ⓓ
24 Ⓕ Ⓖ Ⓗ Ⓙ
25 Ⓐ Ⓑ Ⓒ Ⓓ
26 Ⓕ Ⓖ Ⓗ Ⓙ
27 Ⓐ Ⓑ Ⓒ Ⓓ
28 Ⓕ Ⓖ Ⓗ Ⓙ
29 Ⓐ Ⓑ Ⓒ Ⓓ
30 Ⓕ Ⓖ Ⓗ Ⓙ
31 Ⓐ Ⓑ Ⓒ Ⓓ
32 Ⓕ Ⓖ Ⓗ Ⓙ
33 Ⓐ Ⓑ Ⓒ Ⓓ
34 Ⓕ Ⓖ Ⓗ Ⓙ
35 Ⓐ Ⓑ Ⓒ Ⓓ
36 Ⓕ Ⓖ Ⓗ Ⓙ
37 Ⓐ Ⓑ Ⓒ Ⓓ
38 Ⓕ Ⓖ Ⓗ Ⓙ

39 (grid)

40 Ⓐ Ⓑ Ⓒ Ⓓ
41 Ⓕ Ⓖ Ⓗ Ⓙ
42 Ⓐ Ⓑ Ⓒ Ⓓ
43 Ⓕ Ⓖ Ⓗ Ⓙ
44 Ⓐ Ⓑ Ⓒ Ⓓ
45 Ⓕ Ⓖ Ⓗ Ⓙ
46 Ⓐ Ⓑ Ⓒ Ⓓ
47 Ⓕ Ⓖ Ⓗ Ⓙ
48 Ⓐ Ⓑ Ⓒ Ⓓ
49 Ⓕ Ⓖ Ⓗ Ⓙ
50 Ⓐ Ⓑ Ⓒ Ⓓ
51 Ⓕ Ⓖ Ⓗ Ⓙ

52 (grid)

53 Ⓐ Ⓑ Ⓒ Ⓓ
54 Ⓕ Ⓖ Ⓗ Ⓙ
55 Ⓐ Ⓑ Ⓒ Ⓓ
56 Ⓕ Ⓖ Ⓗ Ⓙ

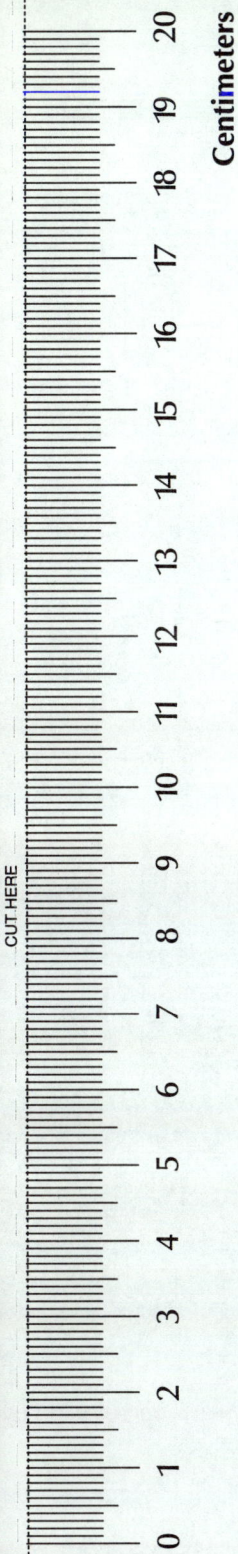

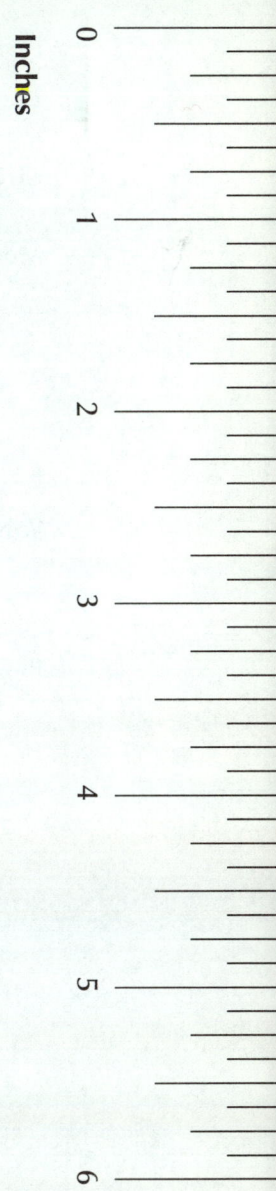

Inches

Centimeters

LENGTH

METRIC

1 kilometer = 1000 meters
1 meter = 100 centimeters
1 centimeter = 10 millimeters

CUSTOMARY

1 mile = 1760 yards
1 mile = 5280 feet
1 yard = 3 feet
1 foot = 12 inches

CAPACITY AND VOLUME

METRIC

1 liter = 1000 milliliters

CUSTOMARY

1 gallon = 4 quarts
1 gallon = 128 ounces
1 quart = 2 pints
1 pint = 2 cups
1 cup = 8 ounces

MASS AND WEIGHT

METRIC

1 kilogram = 1000 grams
1 gram = 1000 milligrams

CUSTOMARY

1 ton = 2000 pounds
1 pound = 16 ounces

TIME

1 year = 365 days
1 year = 12 months
1 year = 52 weeks
1 week = 7 days
1 day = 24 hours
1 hour = 60 minutes
1 minute = 60 seconds

★ CONTINUED on other side…

| Perimeter | square | $P = 4s$ |
| | rectangle | $P = 2l + 2w$ or $P = 2(l + w)$ |

| Circumference | circle | $C = 2\pi r$ or $C = \pi d$ |

Area	square	$A = s^2$
	rectangle	$A = lw$ or $A = bh$
	triangle	$A = \frac{1}{2}bh$ or $A = \frac{bh}{2}$
	trapezoid	$A = \frac{1}{2}(b_1 + b_2)h$ or $A = \frac{(b_1 + b_2)h}{2}$
	circle	$A = \pi r^2$

| Volume | cube | $V = s^3$ |
| | rectangular prism | $V = lwh$ |

| Pi | π | $\pi \approx 3.14$ or $\pi \approx \frac{22}{7}$ |